Plant	Page				
Colchicum, *Naked Ladies*	22, 87			⊝	
Coleus Blumei, *Flame Nettle*	22, 87		⊝		⊟
Commelinas, *Zebrina pendula*	94		⊝		
Conifers – dwarf spp	40	⊟	⊟	⊟	⊟
Convolvulus tricolor	62		⊝		
Cosmos, *Mexican Aster*	87		⊟ ⊝		
Cotoneaster	54	⊟	⊟	⊟	⊟
Courgette	69, 74		▭ ⊟		
Creeping Jenny, *Lysimachia*	22		⊝		
Crocus	21	▭ ⊝			
Cucumber	74		▭ ⊟		
Cup-and-saucer Vine, *Cobaea scandens*	39, 87		⊟		
Cyclamen	38	⊟ ▭ ⊝			
Daffodil, *Narcissus*	63, 87	⊟ ▭ ⊟			
Dahlia	55			▭ ⊟	
Daisy, *Bellis*	85		▭ ⊝		
Dead Nettle, *Lamium*	22, 90		⊝		
Dicentra spectabilis, *Bleeding Hearts*	22, 88		⊝ ⊟		
Dimorphotheca, *Cape Marigold*	54	⊟ ▭ ⊟			
Doronicum, *Leopard's Bane*	62	▭ ⊟			
Eccremocarpus	88		▭		
Echeveria	63		⊟ ▭		
Eleagnus spp	40	⊟	⊟	⊟	⊟
Epimedium	88	▭			
Erica, *Heather*	71, 88		▭ ⊝		
Eucalyptus	40	⊟	⊟	⊟	
Euonymus spp	22, 88	⊝	⊝	⊝	⊝
Euphorbia epithymoides	22, 58	⊝			
Fatsia japonica, *Japanese Aralia*	88	⊟ ⊟	⊟ ⊟	⊟ ⊟	⊟ ⊟
Fern spp	20, 53		▭ ⊝		
Fig	72		⊟		
Flame Nettle, *Coleus*	22, 87		⊝		
Foam Flower, *Tiarella cordifolia*	22		▭ ⊝		
Fuchsia	45, 80, 88		⊟ ▭ ⊝		
Garlic	67		▭		
Gazania, *Treasure Flower*	62		⊟ ⊟		
Geranium, *Pelargonium*	51, 78, 89		⊟ ▭ ⊝ ⊟		
Grape Hyacinth, *Muscari*	21	▭ ⊝			
Grass spp	89		⊝		
Griselinia	63	▭ ⊟			
Gromwell, *Lithospermum*	91		▭ ⊝		
Gypsophila	54		▭ ⊝		
Heather spp, *Erica*	22, 71, 88		▭ ⊝ ⊟		
Hebe spp, *Veronica*	22, 63		⊝		
Hedera spp, *Ivy*	62, 89	⊟ ⊝	⊟ ⊝	⊟ ⊝	⊟ ⊝
Helianthemum, *Sun Rose*	54		▭ ⊝		
Helichrysum petiolatum, *Immortelles*	22, 42		⊝		
Heliotrope, *Cherry Pie*	40		⊝		
Hellebore, *Christmas Rose*	58, 89				▭ ⊟
Helxine, *Mind-your-own-business*	17, 34, 43	⊟ ⊝	⊟ ⊝	⊟ ⊝	⊟ ⊝
Heuchera sanguinea, *Alum Root*	64		▭ ⊝		
Holly	28	⊟	⊟	⊟	⊟

HANGING BASKETS,
WINDOW BOXES & PATIOS

HANGING BASKETS, WINDOW BOXES & PATIOS

by Madge Green

Edited by JIM MATHER
Gardening Editor, The Sunday Mirror

W.Foulsham & Co Ltd
LONDON·NEW YORK·TORONTO·CAPE TOWN· SYDNEY

FOR JOSEPH, WHOSE MOTTO
'MAKE DARK CORNERS BEAUTIFUL'
SEEMS VERY APT FOR THIS BOOK.

W. FOULSHAM & COMPANY LIMITED
Yeovil Road, SLOUGH, Berkshire SL1 4BH

ISBN 0-572-01035-4

Printed in Hong Kong

CONTENTS

Even quite ordinary plants become eye-catchers if raised in some way.

1

PLANTS AND FLOWERS ARE FOR EVERYONE

Container gardening is a delightful pastime, light of heart, lovely, inconsequential. After all, no-one will starve if we don't grow runner beans in our hanging basket, or weep because we chose scarlet zinnias instead of gold calceolarias for the window box. This is something of our own, in which we can simply please ourselves, take intense pleasure and interest, show off, enjoy.

Easy on time and on the eye, its only aim in life is to be charming and give a lift to the day. Seeing our summer hanging basket cascading flowers on a dull rainy day, passers-by may share our delight and perhaps resolve to have a go at something similar themselves. And so we spread the joy.

It is really rather amazing, but the moment we take the most ordinary plant and display it in a window box, a hanging basket, a tub, or an urn, it becomes a plant of some importance, an eye-catcher.

Who first thought of growing plants in containers to display them is unrecorded, though certainly it goes back several thousand years to when the ancient Chinese grew shrubs and other plants in earthenware containers. A queen of Egypt who reigned some 1,500 years B.C. grew plants in pots and sent explorers out to find new subjects, and a carved frieze of small trees in pots adorns her tomb. The Hanging Gardens of Babylon, one of the Wonders of the ancient world, depended largely on plants in porous troughs. Solomon, King of Israel, reputedly a brilliant gardener, was said to have a garden room decorated with many potted plants.

In early times the plants grown in containers were often newly discovered exotic subjects brought by explorers and traders from distant lands, and planted in pots so that they could be brought indoors when protection from bad

A terracotta urn supports an orange tree — circa 1700.

weather was needed. The Romans grew roses in containers to keep them in flower during the winter for use in various festivities, and the Greeks grew things in baskets and other containers as offerings to the gods in the temples.

Royal examples

A very early example of flowers growing in stone troughs in a garden occurs in a painting by an unknown Rhineland artist dating from the early 15th Century and now in a museum at Frankfurt-am-Main; it depicts the Virgin Mary in a walled garden. A famous picture of King Charles II ('The Pineapple Picture', by Henry Danckerts) shows the king in a formal garden which contains large standing pots full of shrubs. Other Royal pictures also feature beautiful plants in large pots and urns as backgrounds; the National Portrait Gallery, for example, has a painting of Prince James Francis Edward Stuart (1688–1766) as a child with his sister. In the background a large terracotta urn supports an orange tree in full blossom – with a parrot sitting prettily on the lower branches.

Incidentally, the word 'greenhouse' is said to come from around the time of the Reformation when it was the thing for the owners of great houses to grow 'tender greens' such as lemons and oranges outdoors in wooden cases or handsome lead or terracotta pots which could be taken inside glasshouses – or 'green houses' – in winter.

Exotic items such as camellias were not thought to be hardy when first introduced to this country, so they were planted in pots and boxes and special houses were built for their protection.

Even tomatoes and runner beans, as newly-introduced novelties, were grown for decoration rather than for food. And at the Palace of Versailles, it is recorded, there were once hundreds of orange trees growing in silver tubs.

Not only the rich, it seems, were attracted to flowers and plants. In Georgian times ragmen in the cities gave potted plants in exchange for old clothes, and a 17th century writer recorded that 'there is scarce an ingenious citizen that by his confinement to a shop, being denied the privilege of having a real garden, but hath his boxes, pots, or other receptacles for flowers, plants, etc.'

An 18th century book on auriculas suggests that the fashion of the day was painting flower pots green, and recommends square pots rather than round. Enthusiasts displayed their potted auriculas on 'stages' in small roofed outdoor 'theatres' or 'buffets' made of wood, the 'backcloth' of the 'stage' being painted black to show off the colours of the flowers.

Still surviving in some gardens of stately homes are such things as vases, boxes, urns, and lead cisterns, mostly dating from the 17th and 18th centuries and all collectors' items if any ever come up for sale. In the 19th century the Victorians loved cast iron garden ware which included all kinds of urns and vases etc. The more expensive wrought iron, fashioned by smiths, was also used to make vases which were like large standing baskets; these were lined with moss, just as hanging baskets are today, before being planted up.

Wirework was popular for vases and baskets; the great 19th century landscape gardener Humphry Repton was fond of wire flower baskets, even using them on lawns.

Mrs. Loudon, the celebrated Victorian writer on gardening, recommends flower baskets in 'The Ladies' Companion to the Flower Garden', written in 1842. Iron baskets, she says, can be on pedestals or else 'appear as if set on the ground', and raised wires can be extended across to support climbing plants. She advises: 'Other receptacles for flowers may be wicker baskets, with the interstices stuffed with moss; or the jars in which grapes have been sent over, but when these last are used, or any other kind of vessel which is very deep in proportion to its breadth, the lower part should be filled with brickbats, pieces of freestone, and other similar materials … in all cases where flowers are grown in baskets and boxes they should stand on a lawn; and the most luxuriant growing kinds should be chosen, to hang down the sides of the vessel.'

She goes on to mention a Captain Mangles, 'whose taste in ornamental gardening is well known', and who suspended baskets from the roof of his greenhouse 'with pots of earthenware or china inside. These baskets are alike suitable for the creeping Cereus, Moneywort, and other common plants which produce their flowers on hanging stems, as for Epiphytes and orchideous plants.'

Mrs. Loudon also suggests the use of wire stands, made up of several tiers, in the conservatory or on the verandah, to hold plants in pots. Her husband, a leading landscape gardener and writer, liked baskets and 'cages' hanging from trees.

Victorian and Edwardian days were perhaps the zenith of container gardening until the present revival of interest, with smart villas and town houses competing with each other in the richness and variety of their hanging baskets, balcony flowers, window boxes, and bulging conservatories. Country people copied and simplified the fashions and so the rustic porch with its hanging basket and the windows full of pot plants came to epitomise the period. There were also many lovely and novel objects around for those who could afford them; for example, special hanging planters which had false bottoms complete with tiny taps to collect and dispose of excess water. Some window boxes had trellis or wire-work arrangements for climbers, and often a hanging basket would be suspended in the centre, all of which must have practically obscured the window!

The Victorians loved doing things in stylish excess; some even went to the trouble of glazing in both sides and front of a window box to form a plant case which sometimes even included a window box aquarium as well as one or more hanging baskets, and which could be heated by a spirit lamp or gas jets and must have looked remarkably attractive at night. Mosses and ferns were grown similarly in 'fernery cases' in sunless windows and houses sometimes had hollow 'fern bricks' built outside a window to hold a fern or other plant.

But with the end of the Edwardian era fashions changed, enthusiasm waned, and window boxes and hanging baskets became 'old hat', while garden urns and pots, as well as the conservatories which once held them, were often left neglected and empty.

Modern trends

Perhaps it was the last war, when every bit of land

A terracotta pot with miniature begonias and nicotiana.

was needed for food production, which brought the small stirrings of a new interest in container gardening for flowers and ornamental plants. I remember as a child in Derbyshire during the war seeing old chimney pots used to grow summer geraniums after the flower garden had been dug up for potatoes. And I well recall seeing, after the war, old 'tin hats' suspended upside down outside the 'prefabs' which were popping up everywhere; they were usually rather sparsely planted with things like catmint or love-in-a-mist.

Most homes today, with their small gardens, or because they have no garden at all, possess at least one plant in a pot, and hanging baskets, window boxes, and patio planters are becoming yearly more popular. A local pottery in my home town, well known for its garden pots, cannot turn them out fast enough to keep up with demand, and a wholesaler friend tells me that whereas hanging baskets were in no demand at all a few years ago, he can hardly get enough of them nowadays.

Growing plants in containers of all kinds makes gardening a possibility for everyone, from the residents of picturesque but hemmed-in cottages such as those of old St. Ives in Cornwall (where I have seen herbs and vegetables as well as flowers in window boxes) to the people on houseboats. Indeed, town dwellers in various parts of the country seem very expert in creating mini-gardens in difficult places, and on a bigger scale local authorities work wonders with tree plantings (often in only a few feet of soil), and beautifully planted boxes, old horse troughs, and so on, in streets and squares.

The City of London has its very own 'hanging gardens' in the new Barbican complex, with over a hundred huge planting 'boxes' supporting forest trees which sometimes have to be planted by crane! It is the City Corporation's admirable policy to acquire any bit of land on which to make a garden, plant a tree, or stand a flower tub, and the idea is certainly catching on in other concrete and glass forests.

All these examples can encourage the average person who wants to create something beautiful, no matter how small the space available, in and around an ordinary house or flat. With enthusiasm and a little know-how you can overcome difficulties and have colourful flowers and refreshing foliage almost all the year round.

The advantages of container gardening for the elderly and handicapped are obvious, and I also particularly like to think of children being encouraged to take an interest in gardening in this way. Planting up a basket or window box with plants bought with pocket money is fun and leads to speedy results which will delight the most impatient child. The secret is to involve the children from the beginning, in choosing the basket or box and deciding what is to be grown. The time to start is spring, when the shops and market stalls are bright with blooms of tempting colours.

Ideas we can copy are everywhere. I am always inspired by the lovely hanging baskets of flowers which seem to be used throughout the City of Bath, for example. Simply keep your eyes open as you go about, to see what local councils are planning, what the bank in the High Street has in its important-looking window boxes, what the shops and hotels have used in their splendid foyer displays of greenery and flowers.

The more we look, the more creative we become, and the more interesting it all is. Even

Fuschia, geranium, begonia and lobelia which will flower all summer.

small towns and villages can teach us things. For summer colour most people would plant up tubs in a pedestrian precinct with geraniums, but in a small town I saw concrete tubs in the streets given an enchantingly different look by massing them with nothing but white marguerites. I aim to copy that on my terrace next year.

2

THE BEAUTY
OF BASKETS

Think of a hanging basket, and I expect you think at once, as indeed most of us do, of an open mesh wire basket of blue lobelia, red or pink geranium, and fuchsia, high in the air. These wire baskets are bought in their thousands every spring and are seen everywhere, with their displays of ... blue lobelia, red or pink geranium, and fuchsia.

In both town and country, local authorities hang them to swing lightheartedly outside the town hall, the swimming baths, the public library, and from the Victorian bandstand in the park, trailing lobelia, geranium, fuchsia. From all the lamp standards in the main streets and along the pedestrian precincts enlightened councils arrange for frivolous riots of ... blue lobelia, geranium, fuchsia, to decorate the summer days. Recognising a good thing when we see it, we tend to copy the lavish, beautifully grown local authority baskets and plant up similar schemes to hang outside our homes.

And so in our sun rooms and outside the little cafe in the High Street, in the porch of the bank, and on the old hook above the solicitors' office, as well as outside the brand new office block, there are our familiar and well-loved lobelia, geranium, and fuchsia cascading from the baskets. All so pretty, so very reliable, so showy, but perhaps – dare I say it? – a tiny bit boring.

Couldn't we try a new scheme, plan a fresh planting, dare a different mixture, or even be very brave and work out a basket for winter effect, or get a crazy idea for spring?

As you are reading this book I expect you are all the way with me in my longing to see many more hanging baskets around the place, but also to see more that are created to be airy delights each with its own particular individuality. So resolved, we will go out to buy our basket ...

To begin with, we obviously need something reliable to hold our flowers aloft nicely, and the sturdy galvanised wire baskets so readily available, sometimes with the wire covered in plastic, really do take some beating and last for years. These won't rust. They can be spray painted, if you like, green, pale blue, or any colour to match your proposed planting scheme or the colour of the house. I use spray-on car body paints (from motor accessory shops) as they are quick to use and cover the wire mesh speedily and easily. A wide range of quick-drying colours is available. However, the basket's growing content should quickly cover all the visible mesh so you may feel it is unnecessary to pay extra for plastic-covered ones or to go to the trouble of painting.

These baskets normally come in three sizes, from 6 inches to big 18-inch ones. If you fancy a really enormous affair you could use one of those big galvanised mesh 'umbrellas' over which are grown standard weeping roses, turning it upside down and hanging it from three strong chains. I have even seen old wire litter baskets, and baskets sold for blanching vegetables, used in this way.

Before deciding on the maxim 'biggest is best', consideration should be given to the weight of the basket when filled with a potting medium plus plants and – something easily forgotten – the weight of water. The added weight in a large quantity of freshly-watered compost can be considerable. Then, too, as plants grow away strongly they weigh a great deal more than they did as youngsters.

Certainly anything off-beat and unusual is attention-getting and interesting in its own right. An occasional Victorian or Edwardian hanging basket is to be found, recognisable by the very attractive decorative shape. Country people have always adapted whatever happened to be handy; I have seen an old log basket, and a wine bottle decanter basket, used to hold a potted plant, also a plastic garden sieve and even half a coconut shell hung up with plants growing directly in them.

Original and useful

Hanging baskets need not necessarily be of wire. They can be of wickerwork and it is quite possible that the first ones were of plaited or woven rush or cane. Deepish baskets with carrying handles, woven from natural materials, can make original and useful containers for use under the cover of a porch, sunroom, etc., hanging from either a beam or a wall. Many interesting baskets are imported nowadays and are easy to find. Fishing, shopping, and bicycle baskets are often seen used cascading flowers from a wall or ceiling, depending on their shape and style. Junk shops and market stalls are well worth searching.

There are many intriguing and beautiful hand-woven baskets around which have been imported from China; they range from variously-sized wicker birdcages to work baskets, hampers, etc,

some with handles or chains. Some are strange shapes whose actual intended use is something of a mystery.

Such baskets made of sea-grass, cane, wicker, and similar natural materials, may well suit both the modern home and the country house where antiques predominate. Of course, they display plants very sympathetically, and they do not mind getting the occasional soaking so long as they are allowed to dry out between-whiles. They can be lined with plastic, or one can put plant pots directly into them. I find the wicker hanging birdcages quite charming for displaying a plant in a pot, in a conservatory or sun room. The round ones in particular are prettier even than the conventional hanging baskets.

White or green plastic-covered wire letter baskets, meant for fixing behind the front door to catch the mail, can be used as wall baskets if provided with a back made from half-inch mesh chicken wire. Lined with plant material such as

moss, they make an effective decoration. Brightly-coloured plastic cutlery drainers, with a hole made in the back for a hook or nail, can look effective if chosen in a colour to match the house.

A macrame string plant holder will hold a half or three-quarters coconut shell just as easily as an expensive small bowl. The shell should have a hole in it for drainage. A matt-textured grey-green succulent or stonecrop can look well against the rough texture of the coconut and the string, a good effect indeed at all times of the year, and especially in harmony with 'cottagey' bow windows or in country gardens hanging from the low branch of a tree.

This reminds me that a friend has a big real shell hanging in her bathroom window, planted up with blue-grey succulents. It is eye-catching against fine curtain nets, and hangs on fishing line which, incidentally, is a marvellous idea for 'invisibly' hanging any container in a window.

Modern buildings in particular look well when hung with plastic hanging containers of 'modern' shape. Generally of soft 'earth' colours, they come in various sizes. They have no drainage holes, so care must be taken with watering and to ensure that they do not become waterlogged with rain. Rather better modern containers do have drainage holes and are supplied with a useful built-in saucer which catches excess water underneath. There are also containers which are completely covered except for holes in the top to take the plants. These last two sorts are a new idea and quite excellent.

It was once thought vital that all growing plants must be in containers with drainage holes. In fact, indoors or under cover of a porch etc. if care is taken over watering drainage holes are not necessary, and I have successfully grown everything from geraniums to exotic bromeliads with no thought to drainage other than the usual bits of broken pot at the bottom.

I was amused recently when I saw a copper kettle hanging in a cottage tea-room, filled with a mass of orange nasturtiums which were growing in a pot hidden inside the kettle. The proprietor told me she had different potted plants coming along all the time, to keep the display in the kettle fresh and attractive. See-through plastic or coloured glass looks sparkling in a window, and I have seen a green plastic ice bucket with a handle showing off dark-foliaged dwarf pink begonias. Some of my own very best effects have been won with the help of some chunky white plastic buckets sold at our local fishmonger's for 10p each. They originally held deliveries of cockles, but hanging from a beam in my conservatory their depth allows me to grow many things from schizanthus (a half-hardy annual, which I allow to trail over the sides) to runner beans (which make a handsome jungly trailing plant), golden hop (another trailer for summer), strawberries, and so on. You do not have to spend a great amount of money on containers – any dish, pot, or vase with handles can be hung just as well as stood, and I have seen keen flower arrangers display pot plants in a hanging piece of suitably-shaped driftwood!

In recent years there has been a fashion for growing woody-stemmed plants such as fuchsias, ivies, geraniums, and even mint, in upturned wine bottles, and many people wonder how it is done. You need a large bottle with a dimple in the bottom, then with a glass cutter or a special bottle cutter you make a round hole in the dimple of

about an inch in diameter. Next cut a strong piece of galvanised wire about 9 inches longer than the bottle and push it right through, hooking one end over the base to secure it and making a hook at the neck end for hanging it up. Holding the bottle upside-down, half fill it with compost, pass a well-rooted cutting through the opening at the base, and you will see that when the bottle is turned the right way up the compost settles down, securing the cutting, which should grow into a fine plant, covering the bottle as it develops up around the sides. Water the plant from the top.

Conversely, some hanging containers have flat bottoms and can be stood instead of hung. They can be filled with plants to stand in an alcove out of doors or on a deep window ledge. Terracotta and stoneware ones look good outdoors, and china, light plastic, etc. indoors.

Flat-backed and other containers of all kinds to hang on walls can be attractive and are, of course, like hanging baskets, space-saving. They can be arranged together in a row or group, or singly, along a wall or trellis, round a door or window, or in a porch. They come in pottery, plastic, metal, basketware, and terracotta, some with holes in the back for hanging, others with built-in baskets, and some with a saucer as part of the hanger. Or an ordinary plant pot can be used by twisting a length of strong wire around it, under the rim, with the ends of the wire formed into a loop for hanging.

A visit to one of those equestrian shops selling bridles, stirrups, etc. can be interesting, for they will have (or be able to get) those marvellous old-fashioned black metal hay racks. They come bow-fronted to fit against a wall or in a corner. They require an extra liner of fine mesh wire netting, and hold lots of moss and plenty of compost. They make handsome decorations for terraces, patios, yards, wide passageways, balconies, sides of garages, or the entrance to a house or flat, and are excellent for places which have no garden at the front other than a paved sunken area. I have also found similar planters on sale at a flower and plant shop and I understand they are available throughout the country. They have a sturdy, pleasing quality and will, I think, become very popular indeed.

While you are in the equestrian shop you may see that they sometimes stock deep green or white plastic feed and water containers designed to hook over the bottom half of a stable door. With a short length of suitably sized pole fixed 'proud' of a wall (this taking the place of the door) you can have an unusual and most useful container for planting, ideal for a houseboat or mobile home garden.

In a porch, hanging baskets do not necessarily need drainage holes.

Happily, now that the idea of hanging plants is in again, many different kinds of container are becoming available, for the market quickly catches up with our requirements, and better things are offered each year, particularly for indoor sunrooms, conservatories, covered balconies and so on, or where some cover such as a porch is available.

From Italy and Spain, pottery hanging containers come in all sorts of shapes, including tub and butter churn shapes, updated versions of a Victorian idea though on the whole far better, being deeper and roomier so that less watering is needed and more plants can be accommodated. They also have the advantage that they don't drip.

They are generally hand-painted underneath and round the sides, with somewhat brightly coloured flowers and leaves and this is a point to watch when choosing them, as it might be difficult to find real plants to tone in colour with the painted ones. Certainly they can look super with matching or toning flowers, but are easiest to use with foliage plants. However, the growing leaves should go with the artist's colours. If the painted leaves are a blue-green try planting up with grey-green ivies, sedums, and such, but if they are yellow-green then lime-green ferns, or the acid-coloured helxine (Mind Your Own Business) will be pleasing and effective.

All kinds of baskets may be pressed into service.

Then there are real baskets of various sizes to take pot plants indoors or in porches and similar situations. They hang from long plaited wickerwork 'chains' and come from the East. The chains are designed for indoor hanging but as temporary decoration for a party a number hung along a verandah or below a balcony, each holding a plant, can be most eye-catching on a still summer evening. They can also be used in a conservatory or sunroom.

Out of doors, real baskets of suitable shape, as well as wire ones, make romantic-looking hangings for garden archways, pergolas, or the bough of a tree. Though real baskets possibly work best when used to hold potted plants rather than actually being planted up themselves. When hanging a basket from a tree branch, by the way, do remember to protect the bark to prevent chafing.

Imagine a stone archway or porch overhung with pale pink roses and underneath it a real basket holding warm pink begonias. Or think of a white clematis over a trellis arch supporting a white wire hanging basket spilling with pale yellow double calendulas. The pots can be placed at different angles by cushioning them in moss.

Ideas are limitless once you start thinking around the subject. One spring, for example, I hung a staggered row of wire mesh baskets the whole length of a very large wedding reception marquee which was lined with blue and white. The moss-lined baskets held pale blue and deeper blue hyacinths, and were caught up with wide ribbons of darker blue and white. On another occasion, for a friend's daughter's wedding I close-planted baskets for the church porch with coleus plants in massed colours to match the

Sometimes antique shops and junk stalls have Edwardian or Victorian hanging pots. Like many available today, they have holes in the top to take wire, ribbon, or cord hangers. I have a matching pair of these cottage window pots; they are a strange pink-red decorated with an embossed acorn design. They are very small and quickly dry out, but are amusing to have. My mother, who is in her eighties, remembers similar hanging pots in the deep cottage windows of her youth. Like mine, she tells me, they hung by three small chains. They were very popular and grew such indoor trailers as campanula isophylla ('Like blue and white stars').

bridesmaids' dresses and bouquets. The effect was very novel and much admired, and afterwards the bride enjoyed the plants in patio pots at her new home.

A point worth remembering always is that a basket should never be hung so high that it cannot be reached easily for either watering, tending, or taking up or down. However, if for some reason you find you must hang a basket sky-high a stepladder or a handy bedroom window can come in useful! A rafter or beam is best for hanging a basket from a ceiling or in a porch or conservatory, and this is simply a matter of a strong hook screwed into firm wood. Stanley Garden Tools make a swivel hook which allows baskets to be swivelled round so that plants get the light; it is available in brass or black finish.

If a basket is to be hung out from a wall an arm or bracket support, in wood or metal, is required and this must be attached to the wall very firmly by means of screws and wall plugs (such as Rawlplugs and similar makes). Special hanging brackets are available in the shops; the metal ones not only look decorative but are strong and lasting and usually have a hook on which the basket can be hung. Types in which basket and bracket are permanently fastened together have the disadvantage that, once fixed to the wall, the basket cannot be easily removed for replanting or other attention.

Make them safe

People must be able to pass safely under your basket, and if either a basket or window box is to be over any kind of pathway, pavement, road, or patio, make doubly sure that it is safely fixed.

Just well-grown geraniums look very pretty when displayed like this.

Don't skimp on buying hooks that really are large enough and strong enough. If the hook screws too easily into a beam, for instance, it may well be that there is wood rot present. All hanging chains, wires, screws, and other supports, brickwork, stucco, and woodwork should be checked yearly without fail to see that all is still safe, for things deteriorate. A good idea is to use two hooks instead of one.

Many people like to hang a basket above a window so that it can be seen from inside the house, but do be careful about this. Gales can blow up at all times of year and a site you thought was sheltered can become a windy whirlpool, making your basket into a wind-driven battering

When fully grown, the plants should conceal the moss completely.

ram. A friend of mine had a large sitting room window broken by a basket which ran amok! It is worth experimenting with the empty basket, to see how much room it needs to swing in, before planting and installing it.

Select a spot for hanging any kind of basket with care. It is folly, for instance, to place a basket of delicate ferns on the corner of the house where it will be subject to constant winds. Indeed, a windy site is very difficult and if possible should be avoided. Wind is possibly even worse than sunshine for drying out a basket almost before you have turned your back on it. If you must plant in a draughty spot, choose subjects such as stonecrop, sedums, plectranthus, or geraniums, which will put up with a certain amount of ill-treatment. Most ferns require a moist, still atmosphere to do really well, and a north facing aspect may be chosen.

Don't always go the way of the crowd – be original. Smaller houses are cosy and intimate and it is nice to be able to look into our baskets, get to know them and enjoy them, so wall baskets can be placed at eye level. It is pleasant as we go to put the key in the door to discover, for example, that many quite ordinary annual flowers (e.g., some petunias) are deliciously scented. I always put a few wallflowers in my little conservatory, in a nose-high wall basket, and enjoy weeks of their scented company. You don't have to be rich to feel rich!

By placing mirrors opposite or just behind a hanging basket you can give the effect of masses of expensive profusion at no extra cost. A canework tray placed behind a wall basket makes a good setting for plants, giving them an added importance and impact and creating a neat picture for the centre of a plain wall.

All climbers and such things as ordinary geraniums and fuchsias as they mature will trail as well as climb if not supported, and often look more naturally at home, and certainly different, if allowed to fall gently over the rim of the basket, rather than being pinned up to sticks or twisted round wires. Most baskets need trailers, and some good ones include ajuga (bugle), ivies, tradescantia, and columnea.

Another means of getting an original look is to plant up baskets to colour-match window boxes and terrace pots. And a basket of one sort of plant in mixed or matching colours can be most effective, in that it is less usual and achieves a look of having been planned.

In choosing plants for baskets there is a wide range of hardy and half-hardy subjects; the hardy ones making permanent plantings with all-year-round interest possible. I always have a number of my own baskets planted up with suitable hardy border plants such as the variegated periwinkle, perennial pansies (viola cornuta), dwarf campanulas, and violets. Some of my most attractive baskets are simply made up of mixed foliage plants.

For permanent indoor decoration or for summer out of doors, baskets of maidenhair fern are attractive and other plants I use are fittonia, peperomia, pilea, chlorophytum, ceropegia (a trailing succulent from Africa) and chenille plant (acalypha hispida).

I generally leave a space in the centre of any hanging basket to take the odd flowering pot plant, for it is amazing how, when a basket has been looking fabulous and spilling flowers as if they would never stop blooming, it suddenly decides to take a rest as soon as I invite visitors round. At Christmas I sometimes add extra colour with a scarlet ribbon bow (there is a waterproof ribbon available for outdoors), and berried holly.

No matter what the time of year, it should never be necessary to use plastic flowers in a hanging basket – here are just a few ideas:
Spring: Basket lined with moss or arenaria balearica, thyme, or any suitable low-growing alpine plant; top planted with pansies, double daisies, golden alyssum; small bulbs such as muscari, crocus, scilla, and puschkinia planted in the sides and top; larger bulbs such as hyacinths and dwarf tulips in the top only. For the top and

An amusing and imaginative mix of things.

for sprawling over the edge try euphorbia epithymoides with its splendid yellow-green flowers and bracts and grey snakey leaves, plain or gold foliage lysimachia (creeping Jenny), anthemis cupaniana (fine grey foliage with white flowers), tiarella cordifolia (the foam flower, with heart-shaped leaves and white foaming flowers). For very large baskets, dicentra spectabilis is superb, with its pink dangling heart-shaped flowers and pretty foliage.

Summer: Lining as for spring, or you can use dwarf campanula. Basket planted up with tuberous and fibrous rooted begonias, and the

Baskets can be lined with materials other than moss or plastic. Arenaria balearica, the 'spilt milk plant' always looks rich and green.

pendulous varieties which have an obvious application to hanging baskets; all kinds of geraniums, fuchsias, petunias, nasturtium, marigold, coleus, Busy Lizzie, (impatiens), ajuga (bugle), schizanthus (poor man's orchid), campanula isophylla, helichrysum petiolatum, or almost any suitable-looking hardy or half-hardy plant lifted from the garden, bought from a nursery, or raised from seed (not forgetting trailing lobelia).

Autumn: Lining as for spring and summer. Planted with dwarf chrysanthemum, autumn crocus and colchicum (the double purple colchicum Water Lily is particularly striking); these should be removed from the basket before their huge spring foliage arrives. Try also arum italicum pictum, an especially handsome hardy plant with orange berries and patterned green arrow-like leaves as interesting as any exotic indoor plant, and any low-growing variegated foliage shrubs such as euonymus.

Winter: Lining as above, or with plain or variegated arabis, violets, thrift, or any alpine with good close foliage. Top planted with winter-flowering heathers or heathers with colourful winter foliage, young plants of hebe armstrongii with its khaki-coloured foliage, arum italicum pictum, lamium maculatum (its hanging foliage has a silvery stripe), the grey woolly foliage stachys lanata, tiarella (pink-green leaves in winter), saxifrage (silver encrusted rosettes), and sempervivum (houseleek, in many colours).

3

EYE-CATCHING WINDOW BOXES

My very first window box began life as a wooden tomato basket with a metal handle and the words 'Best Guernsey' printed across it in red. My husband took off the handle, sanded down the rough wood to a finer finish, and gave the outside a coat of primer then two coats of crisp white paint. We treated the inside with wood preservative and made holes for drainage.

I was very impatient to instal it and almost before the paint was dry had dashed into town and chosen three perfect scarlet geraniums to match the red and white checks of the kitchen curtains. By the time my husband was home from the office I had the box filled with garden soil and my plants in situ. I was very young!

That weekend we screwed a couple of shelf brackets on to the kitchen window sill and hoisted the box into position. The soil-filled box was quite heavy, and in raising it we broke off two of the flower heads. Because we had not given it sufficient thought, the box was positioned in such a way that opening the window proved impossible, but being newly married I didn't like to say so and suffered an over-hot kitchen all summer. Each time it rained, earth from the box was splashed on the window, and soil washed out through the drainage holes.

The site was windy, much watering was required, and on occasion my unstaked plants blew over, but apart from these teething troubles

A smart town window box has petunias, ivy and trailing asparagus.

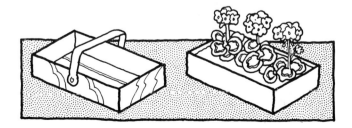

A nice touch — bringing the garden into the porch.

the window box gave us great pleasure and was much admired. It lay fallow and slightly depressing all winter, until it blossomed again in the spring when it was planted with long-stemmed daffodils. That first window box gave me a taste for container gardening and taught me a lot. Since then I have had many boxes, not all of them directly under the windows. I use them a

great deal nowadays in a glass porch. We have widened the small ledges on either side to make them deep enough to carry the boxes, and I have other boxes standing on the floor. They are all enchanting every bit of the year with sweet-scented hyacinths after Christmas followed by such things as mixed primroses and polyanthus, with pansies later and then geraniums.

I choose geraniums with fancy foliage so that they are pleasing even when out of bloom. I have a number of boxes coming along all the time, which I recommend if at all possible, so that the effect is always bright and fresh. From the lane the whole porch looks like a small glass jewel box sparkling with colour, and in the dark winter months when the welcoming porch light goes on the effect is specially magical. Plants grow well within the protection of the glazed sides and door, and I am even able to get my geraniums safely through the winter as we are in a fairly frost-free very high and windy situation, facing south.

Change-over boxes

It is good to have a number of interchangeable window boxes so that jaded, faded plantings can be removed as they go over and be exchanged for fresh plants just coming up to their best. These need not necessarily be expensive – look around and see what you can find in the way of boxes. For instance, butchers often have empty white plastic boxes which can be ranged together in a row. The cockle buckets in plastic which I get from my fishmonger to use as hanging containers, as described in the chapter on hanging baskets, can be used equally well in window box situations. For this purpose I wash them out, remove the handles, and make holes in the bottom. Three or four together along a ledge are quite expensive-looking and make perfect containers for growing flowers, herbs, or even things such as lettuces and strawberries. At the front of the house they display neat arrangements of marguerites or petunias.

However, it is not always possible to find space for accommodating a number of replacement boxes, and in that case it is necessary to replant existing boxes more often, or else go in for permanent plantings.

Although it will be easier if I talk about window boxes, box-shaped plant holders can be placed in many different places around the outside of a house, not only immediately outside windows. The great advantage of the window position is, of course, that we can enjoy the flowers from indoors. Plain walls close to front or back doors make very suitable places for hanging boxes, however, and often a dull garage wall will prove to be an ideal spot. Sometimes garages are attached to the house but project forward a little way, so forming a cosy L-shaped alcove which nicely shelters the front door. This is a superb place for a wall-hung box and creates a note of greeting.

A plain wall which faces on to a wide walkway or a balcony outside a town flat simply asks for one or more boxes, perhaps on each side of the door. Indeed, you can make your front wall into a veritable hanging garden with a number of boxes or baskets glowing with colourful leaves and flowers.

Choosing the site of a window box is clearly very important. For instance, they are often best in uncluttered surroundings, not hemmed in by

Again, bringing the country to town using cascading ivies.

garden plants growing too close. Any spot we pass daily as we come and go is good; in such a place we can not only enjoy our box all the time but also do a bit of speedy weeding or dead-heading as we pass and, most important of all, we can easily see when the box needs watering.

Windows with deep ledges of stone or tile will accommodate boxes easily, and shelter the plants from the worst of wind and weather. So close to the house, they are often warm enough to risk planting out frost-tender subjects slightly earlier than with boxes which hang on the outside of a bow window, for example, where they are open to the elements with little protection.

There are other things about the siting of a window box to which one perhaps does not at first give a thought. Being human, we choose a fine bright day to go outside and put up a box. Few consider whether the box will face north or south, whether the site is open to the prevailing wind, whether the building has deep eaves which will shelter the box from the rain, and so on.

The wise, however, will work with their individual situation. Handsome boxes can be contrived for every aspect, but if there is a choice we should pick a spot which receives good light and has the possibility of sunshine for at least part of the day if we want to grow flowering plants or foliage plants with brightly coloured leaves. Green-leaved plants will put up with shade and flag more quickly in a hot or windy place.

Many tall modern buildings seem to funnel the wind round themselves, creating strong airflows even on otherwise calm days. This can be a real problem to the window box gardener and make hanging baskets even more difficult, for wind is drying (perhaps even more than sunshine) and rapidly takes moisture from the soil. If you have such a site and cannot fix up any kind of wind filter such as a bit of fine trellis on each side, or even bamboo stakes placed fairly close together to form an interesting-looking shield, it might be best to cut your losses and take your window box indoors.

Indoor boxes, in sunrooms etc., are very easy to manage and can be filled with geraniums, begonias, succulents and any of the wide variety of house plants now available, or with pots of ageratum, French marigold, streptocarpus, etc.

A window box outside the kitchen window, like my own very first one, is a pleasant way of helping along the daily kitchen chores by giving something colourful at which to look. A permanently planted box can also form a screen to give privacy indoors – plants are far more interesting than curtain nets, and block out far less light than the half-drawn curtains many people favour.

I think that even against a frosted-glass window a box full of colourful subjects has a part to play, as bold scarlets, bright blues, yellow, orange, and white shine through from outside. Boxes may be hung under the window as well as actually on the ledge so preventing soil splashing on windows; with a light trellis bordering the window to carry climbers the effect can be quite countryfied. Even the gardenless can grow sweet peas in a deep hanging box or tub against the wall. With either wooden or plastic-covered metal trellis you can grow clematis, climbing roses, or honeysuckle round the door. Really the sky is the limit!

Window boxes can be constructed or bought to fit any size, type, or style of window, even the curved bays and bows which are still as popular as ever they were. You can place one long box or three shorter ones at the centre front of a five-section bay window, leaving the outer sections free to open, or you can have a separate box for each section. The easiest way is to make these of wood, covering the joins and linking them into one sleek whole with a long piece of pliable hardboard or thin plywood nailed into place and

painted to match the house. With this method only the simplest of boxes are required but the stronger they are the better when it comes to fixing the linking facia board.

Even a french door need not defeat the keen window box gardener. I once saw two boxes attached one each to the bottom woodwork of a pair of french doors. The hotelier owner, a keen do-it-yourself man, had fitted the boxes with particularly strong supports underneath and at the sides to take the weight. The doors were in constant use, and the flower-filled boxes, moving with the doors, caused much interest.

An idea I like is to use a wall or fence in the garden to support hanging boxes; this is especially pleasing with the boundary wall of a patio or terrace. Where there is a rise of level in the garden it is often possible to build a low retaining wall with a flat top to hold boxes. Similarly, a swimming pool or garden pond can have a backing of well-planted boxes or tubs.

Any flat roof, such as a garage or the top of a bay window, will take a long window box and look attractive with flowers hanging down. A white box or one painted to match the house looks as good above a window as below, and the effect of a short light curtain of flowers or leaves can be achieved if trailing plants are chosen. Balconies with railings will also allow the installation of boxes for trailing plants.

Of course, some provision must be made for watering. It is a nuisance if a ladder or stepladder is needed every time a box has to be watered (and very regular watering is necessary where boxes are mounted high and open to sun and wind). Often if the box is suitably placed it can be watered from an upstairs window with the aid of a long-spouted

watering can. The more prominently a box is sited, the more it needs to look always well-cared-for and attractive.

Planted boxes often look exceptionally well near a front door, perhaps on wide steps leading up to the door or on flat piers either side. Here a collection of one sort of plant – perhaps houseleeks, ivies, or even cacti in summer – make an effective display by being raised and presented to view in this way. Another idea is to plant neatly clipped golden privet or box, or holly. You could even go in for a bit of topiary!

A clever gardening friend of mine displays her collection of fine fuchsias each summer on home-made wooden staging – shelves of varying heights and widths – under her dining room window. This is a wonderful idea for showing off a number of interesting plants together where space is at a premium. I display plants in my conservatory in the same way, using old metal display units from shops. Painted white, they look rather like

expensive Victorian ware. One cost me 50p, the other was given to me after I had seen it outside the shop when it was waiting to be collected by the dustmen. The kind of metal staging sold for greenhouses could be similarly painted and used outdoors. The aluminium kind won't rust.

Complement the building

At all times window boxes and other containers should be chosen to marry up with the building on which they are displayed. Perhaps the best window boxes, like the best cut flower containers, are unobtrusively in keeping with the plants and the surroundings. A mock 18th century lead box (glass fibre copy) embossed with sporting wood nymphs or something similar would look out of place on a modern glass and concrete building, but plain shapes, even plastic ones, in quiet colours fit in anywhere.

In some instances, however, buildings with a strong character of their own are made even more interesting by an off-beat choice of window box. I know an angler who has wickerwork fishing baskets spilling flowers along the window sills of his old cottage by a river, and in a cathedral city I noticed a box faced with pottery tiles depicting English cathedrals. The tiles were designed in donkey brown on white, and the woodwork of the house was a matching gentle shade of chocolate. The box itself was bright with marigolds and the effect was memorable.

In a small country town I saw a window box gaily painted in blue with a white heart design, and nearby a planted box hanging by the side of the door had the house number painted on it – practical as well as unusual. The number itself, by the way, was fashioned from thick cord tacked into position and then painted. A house named Pen Cottage had a deep window box decorated with a metal replica of a quill pen.

They say every house and garden should have at least one memorable feature, and even if you have no garden a window box could be such a feature. Happily there is the very widest possible choice of containers about nowadays. You can take your pick from every shape and size, wood or plastic, plain or fancy, real antique or mock. Certainly there is something available to suit every style of home, from modern flat to country cottage. Whatever the depth of our purse, however, the first consideration must be the size – and especially the depth – of the window box.

A deep box will always be more practicable than a shallow one, which has too little room for the roots of most plants and also quickly dries out. Even if we plan to use the box simply as a means

of holding a row of plants in pots the effect is less attractive if the pots all stick up above the rim. The old adage 'Buy the best you can afford' does not necessarily apply, for the most expensive may be totally out of keeping with the property. Wooden window boxes may be fairly easily made by the average handyman and can be painted or stained. Here more expenditure will certainly result in a better job, for the better the wood the better the box will be. Hardwood or cedar is obviously better than old orange boxes!

Don't use creosote on a window box – plants do not care for it. Instead use a proprietary wood preservative, with two coats worked well into the joints. If they take your fancy, you can decorate the front of a window box with stick-on plastic motifs in such designs as Georgian swags. Or you can make your own decorations with such pretty and interesting things as seashells, horse shoes, or coloured glass.

Expanded polystyrene troughs or boxes make a wonderfully comfortable home for plants. Unfortunately I have not seen these in full-scale window box sizes recently, though I have some which are about ten years old. I paint them every year to keep them spick and span. These polystyrene boxes are always warm to the touch, even on cold days. Many electrical goods and other household items are packed nowadays in moulded boxes of polystyrene to protect them during transit. Shops will often give you these moulded shapes to save throwing them away and over the years I have collected many and used them as plant boxes or seed boxes. Some are in unusual shapes, some have recessed circles or squares which make a decoration, and when painted they look like expensive sculptured creations. Ordinary gloss or emulsion paints can be used to colour them. A fault with polystyrene (possibly why it is not apparently used for big window boxes any more) is that it is brittle and needs careful handling. Any plant container in this material should be placed in position before being filled with compost. It is easy to bore holes through the back or sides for wires or cords which can be secured to hooks in the window frame to keep the box in position.

Wooden window boxes are traditional cottage fare with a decoration of tree bark. Nowadays we can buy pieces of interestingly-textured cork bark sold by florists for flower arrangers' use. It is rubbery and seems almost indestructible. I like, too, the white picket fence effect sometimes seen on window boxes in the countryside. And how about this for a really splendid idea? – On holiday in Devon I saw a rowing boat secured, upright, to a wall, with the seats supporting pots of scarlet geraniums!

Window boxes could, of course, be suitably shaped baskets, fitted with some kind of lining to hold the compost and prevent its dampness rotting the wickerwork. I have managed to keep some of my baskets for ten years by lining them with polythene and spray painting them both inside and outside. Flowers and plants do however always have a look of the country when seen against the texture and quiet colour of a basket left in its natural colour, undoubtedly giving distinction and originality to any window. Plastic baskets sold for various household purposes are often suitably shaped to become practical 'window boxes'. Baskets of all kinds are easily kept safely in place by passing a length of wire through the weave and securing the ends to

Above: A jolly, green home-made window box. Notice the wedges to lift and provide easy drainage.

Opposite: A beautifully schemed summer box of unobtrusive white plastic which harmonises well with the house.

ring eyelets screwed into the wooden window sill or frame.

Going to the other extreme, you can spend a lot of money on genuine old lead window boxes which can sometimes be bought at country house sales or from antique dealers. Unless well secured they could tempt thieves to lift them from your wall, but less easy to steal are antique or modern terracotta, concrete, stone (or mock stone) troughs, sinks, urns, and so on, which are particularly suitable for old houses with deep windows and strong ledges. They look equally handsome standing free on the ground outside a large window, where their shape is seen to advantage.

The antique look can be obtained more cheaply with the very attractive glass fibre, aluminium, cast iron, etc., boxes now available. They are often moulded replicas of very old patterns, though recently I have noticed some less heavily decorated ones in the shops. Glass fibre is very strong, light, and weather-resistant and these boxes should last for years with the minimum of attention.

With any mock antique box it is a good idea to go for a really old appearance. I rub mine all over with clods of really wet earth. Lightly brush off the ·earth; some will remain in the cracks, crevices, or rough surface texture and help to give a patina of age. Placed in a shady spot, the box will acquire its own moss or lichen.

Useful self-watering planters can be bought nowadays. Made of plastic, they employ various methods to keep the plants watered automatically for as long as three or four weeks. Apart from helping the forgetful, these planters can also be a protection against the fault of over-watering, as they are designed to control the amount of water the plants receive. Although meant primarily for indoor plants, I see no reason why they should not be used for window boxes, and possibly the principle will be extended to bigger boxes.

Turning again to ideas from the past, I have seen old-fashioned iron fire grates and hearth curbs fitted to window sills, painted, and thus making attractive settings for a display of plants. If you don't have anything like this in the attic, a blacksmith would make you something similar – perhaps a simple plain iron band to fix above the sill and in front of a box or a row of pots. Again, a blacksmith would make decorative iron brackets to hold up a heavy window box, in place of the ordinary shop-bought kind which are usually practical rather than specially good to look at.

4

PATIO POTS, URNS & THINGS

Very closely allied to the hanging basket and window box is a wide range of containers in which to grow flowers and shrubs etc. to grace the terrace, patio, yard, or entrance-way, a flat roof, a balcony, a wall or a sunroom. The right container can even be used indoors and I have used an urn made of stone on a plinth showering ivies and trailing geraniums in a large window to great effect.

Well planted containers around the vicinity of the house encourage always a warm and welcoming feeling. And there is no lack of different shapes and sizes from which to choose. They can, for example, if we place them properly create a light screen for a window, a garden seat, or a barbecue area, filter the wind, and bring a delicate touch of country green to a city home. But one of their best attributes, from the busy person's point of view, is that they are always close at hand and tending them is as easy and natural as admiring them.

I have a fair number of outdoor containers collected over the years. They range from old stone sinks and the largest sizes of commercial plant pots to a decorated terracotta urn reputed to have once belonged to Lord Baden-Powell, the founder of Scouting. There is a jar which I bought when I was first married, made from a piece of stone after the bombing of the Houses of Parliament during the war, and bearing an inscribed plaque to prove it! Then there is a mock-bronze urn, a huge Victorian pot so large that it is made in two halves (and it takes two people to lift each half). Various big pottery bread-making crocks have proved surprisingly frost-hardy. Two fairly plain earthenware urns came from a local pottery, and in splendid contrast are my two genuine Georgian terracotta mock baskets complete with pretty handles.

I am always moving them around, sometimes as I make other changes in the garden, sometimes (when they are replanted) in order to make them fit more pleasingly into their immediate environment. At my last home, where we had no grass, only paved areas, I found my various pots and troughs particularly useful, dotted along the paths, at the end of vistas on terraces, by the pool, and in the rose garden and borders. In my present garden they are used in a similar way to give emphasis and interest wherever a kind of visual 'punctuation mark' is needed. Like good paving or smooth lawns, a well-shaped pot or other container of pleasing proportions gives a feeling of repose and order, especially where there are 'busy' multi-coloured flower borders or the confused patterning of lots of green foliage. If the pots are empty during the cold months they still manage to add interest and a gentle solidity to the winter garden. As you see, I am very fond of my containers!

I find that patio and terrace pots and tubs are often interchangeable with window boxes. It is interesting to buy varying sizes of the same kind of container, or various shapes in the same material, to arrange together in a cluster, a row, or a tier, as well as to display individually. A tiered group is always effective, with the tallest of the

New life for an old chimney pot. Imaginative and nicely placed.

into the cracks and crevices of paving, where it would soon go rampaging away and become a nuisance.

Containers display their plants best if raised off the ground, perhaps just on a couple of bricks (which helps drainage) or to window sill level. Wood, metal, or stone staging can be used in a suitable position, perhaps against a wall, or stone or brick pillars in a more conspicuous position. One or more suitably sized pieces of a sturdy tree trunk can look effective, and incredibly versatile are those open concrete building blocks, in various designs, sold for making decorative garden walls, loggias, and so on. They have an airy, lively effect when built up to form square or oblong plinths and pillars. They are not heavy to lift and move, and if the structure is not too high or too complex it is not necessary to cement them together. There are also interlocking bricks which can be used in a variety of ways. A trip round the local builders' merchant or garden centre will provide many ideas and (usually) illustrated pamphlets. I found one of my favourite plinths in a wood where someone had thrown it away; it is simply the drum of an old washing machine!

Lengths of glazed drainpipes, which come in various widths, can be very good for supporting containers, and will even make containers themselves. I remember visiting a garden in which a number of such pipes, of different sizes, were placed together to form a sort of upright sculpture on a terrace. All kinds of trailing ivies were planted in them. I thought this such a good idea that I copied it.

I like, too, the tower pots which one sees in shops and garden centres as planters for herbs and strawberries. The individual pots, in

group at the back and the smallest at the front, with each pot spilling its flowers into the one below. Trailing lobelia, usually seen in hanging baskets and window boxes, can look entrancing when used in this manner, as can mind-your-own business, which trickles down as a mossy green cascade from one container to another. One should beware of letting this latter plant escape attractive plastic, are locked together to form a pillar or tower, with 'balconies' at intervals all the way up to take the plants. They are suitable for both indoors and outdoors. Using modern plastic materials like this has made many such interesting and relatively inexpensive containers available. Few of us can afford the antique wine jars, Moorish pots, Roman storage jars, and the like, which we may admire on holidays abroad. However, many of the classic shapes or very similar ones are still being produced by modern potters and are worth looking out for. Junk shops are not what they were for turning up treasures, for much of what used to be junk is now 'antique' and expensive; nevertheless, market stalls, backstreet shops, and builders' yards do at times provide something useful and rare.

Look for a bargain

Towards the end of the summer lots of nurserymen and garden centres clear out their old stock at bargain prices. I have bought many a container at less than full price after pointing out some chip or flaw or missing bit to the salesman; after all, any such imperfection can be covered with a trailing plant. I always think that a damaged handle, for instance, takes the newness off and possibly makes a container look older and more interesting. In search of a tough and inexpensive container, I have often found something in an office equipment shop – a sensibly sized plastic wastepaper bin. These come both round and square, and if you don't like the colour (offices seem to go in for very bright shades nowadays) they can be painted. Holes must be made in the bottom if for use outdoors.

An elegant container looks even better when seen with other classic shapes.

Old stone sinks make marvellous containers for alpines. If the sink is rather shallow it can be made deeper by cementing irregular pieces of stone or rock all the way round the rim, or along the sides and back only so that a miniature mountain slope is formed when the sink is filled with soil or compost. Alpines need good drainage, so cover the bottom of the sink with broken crocks, not forgetting to cover the plug hole with a piece to prevent it becoming blocked with soil. Tilting the whole sink very slightly, so that the plug hole is at the lower end, is a good idea.

A simple box garden – a deep, narrow, rectangular box built of brick or stone, like a hollow wall – makes an excellent container for growing all kinds of plants. Sited close to the house along a terrace, down the drive, or to form a boundary to a lawn, a box garden can be an impressive architectural feature in the garden. I once saw such a garden used to hide the dustbins of a block of flats. Apart from the open planting area at the top, the wall can have small openings or crevices in its vertical surfaces to take trailing plants.

Though I have talked about boxes, tubs, and so on, I take plant containers to mean almost anything which can be planted up, looks decorative or interesting, and can withstand the weather. One of my favourites in this category is my little Victorian child's wheelbarrow, which makes a charming setting for mixed spring flowers and summer pansies. Every winter it is carefully emptied, dried out, and given a fresh coat of wood preservative. Before refilling and replanting in spring it is lined with a sheet of plastic to help protect the timber.

Real garden wheelbarrows, especially the now rather old-fashioned wooden kind, make excellent containers, with the great additional advantage that they are easy to move around. A barrow which has seen its best days after years of ordinary garden use can go into honourable retirement, like one which for many years I saw brought out each season and proudly placed on its owner's front lawn, suitably planted up. It signalled the beginning of summer for me. Incidentally, making drainage holes seems unnecessary – old wooden wheelbarrows always leak!

Mobility is, to my mind, one of the particular joys of container gardening. We can move things around the garden or patio as the whim takes us. Containers whose plants are at their best can go into prominent positions, while those which have gone out of flower are moved out of the limelight. Lilies just breaking bud may be a feature one month, a scarlet rose in a tub may take over the star spot the following month, and so on.

Always aim for the big effect if you can – containers planted in a meagre manner never look right. One really well-planted container will always look better than several sparse or half-empty ones. A good rule is to find tall, eye-catching subjects for the centre of the planting, trailers to flow over the edges, and in between, shapes and colours to link the two. On very windy sites, however, it may be wise to keep to low-growing subjects. Very tall urns and tubs look effective with a good tuft or finial at the top – an evergreen yucca, for instance – with a simple edging round the rim of, say, trailing fuchsias.

All containers look well when displayed on an area of paving, gravel, or stone chippings. The style of your house and garden needs to be taken into account and, of course, the cost. Just a few paving slabs, however, can be used under a group of containers to set them off without the expense of paving a larger area. Plain grey or stone-coloured slabs and chippings usually look better than the highly-coloured kinds. Picturesque and economical, if you live in an area where they abound naturally, are flints or pebbles set in

concrete, and if you can get hold of enough old bricks they too can be laid as paving or built up to form simple plinths for tubs and urns.

Taking the idea of paving a little further, a paved area can become a courtyard garden, with sheltering walls of brick or garden building blocks, and the perfect setting for container gardening. The additions of a simple pool, even a fountain, can be really effective. Containers can also be set around a sunken area, so that the flowers and plants are seen almost at eye level. Difference in levels is always attractive in a garden, and containers of all kinds make it easy to achieve this.

Lilies in containers

One of the most pleasing aspects of pot gardening is that it allows us to grow many desirable things which might otherwise be denied us because of the nature of our garden soil. For instance, if the soil is not suitable for all the lovely range of lime-haters such as azaleas, camellias, rhododendrons, etc., our larger tubs and pots can be filled with suitable lime-free compost to suit them, and we can give them good drainage too. I have found this is the very best way of growing lilies, for in the confines of a deep container I can provide them with the right soil (three parts good loam, one part peat, and two parts coarse sand) and keep them free from their deadly enemies the slugs. And there is no danger of sticking a fork right through them during the months they are under cover below the surface. As with most plants, a pot displays them beautifully, so that they appear like a magnificent growing flower arrangement.

In spring, patio pots can make a fine home for dwarf hardy cyclamen or any bulbs large and small, different pots being brought into view as others 'go over', or else if we have only one permanent pot the bulbs can be removed and replanted in the garden to die down. Last year I was impressed by a matched planting of window boxes, and terrace pots; all were planted richly and thickly with the same blue scillas. The white walls of an old timbered cottage made the perfect setting. Later in the year, hardy fuchsias took over the flowering; their slim bare branches had not been noticeable in the spring. Pure white Christmas roses are a delight in the porch at the home of one of my friends from December onward, and sweet-scented osmanthus near the doorway is another idea to bring a quiet pleasure to a cold day in early spring.

Although you can grow almost anything you fancy in a pot, most people settle for summer geraniums or annuals. Do, I urge you, explore the wide field of hardy plants. A good nurseryman's catalogue is invaluable when deciding what to grow. One of my favourites, which I consider the perfect plant for any outdoor pot, is the ordinary garden form of sedum spectabile. This makes an interesting plant at all times of the year. Its grey-green succulent leaves come early, studding the pot with low rosettes which continue growing right through spring and into summer, when they begin to show their flat fresh green closely-clustered heads of buds and then the flowers, which mostly open pink. Sedum spectabile Autumn Joy is particularly good, giving more richly-coloured flowers. Mass the plants very close. I leave the old flowerheads on through the winter, for they really do look like chocolate-brown flowers, cutting them off when they begin to get raggy and worn by the early spring. There is a lovely green and pale yellow variegated sort listed by some nurseries and a purple-bronze finer leafed form which is not quite so good alone in a pot but mixes well with a yellow, green, or white colour scheme.

A novel idea, even for a balcony, is to take a very big tub and make in it a tall 'wigwam' of bamboo canes, tied together at the top with rot-proof string or wire and then grow tomatoes or runner beans up them, or else Cobaea scandens (the cup and saucer vine), climbing nasturtiums, or Ipomoea Heavenly Blue whose great trumpets of flowers open fresh every morning. Such a tub looks well on top of a coal bunker or dustbin shelter, if there is absolutely nowhere else to site it.

Any container can be used to create a miniature scenic garden, if that sort of thing appeals. Small shrubs may be used to suggest trees, rocks become mountains, and the tiny leaves and flowers of dwarf alpines are in scale. It could be pleasing to grow bonsai trees in such a situation. A light covering of fine stone chippings,

Many indoor plants like to be outdoors during the summer.

gravel, or peat tidies up the top of an open pot and makes it look cared-for. Small pebbles or shells from the seaside not only look good around a potted dwarf conifer in a cottage garden setting, for instance, but they also have the advantage (like gravel and chippings) of keeping the soil a little moist in summer. A popular hobby at the moment is painting real pebbles with scenes or pictures of birds, flowers, etc., and these can be amusing standing on the gravel along with shells or perhaps small coloured glass fishing net floats. Women have always enjoyed linking decorative items with pot plants and it is good to continue this.

nose level from a deckchair in the sun, and with container gardening we do have time to sit in the sun among our growing things.

Many young trees and shrubs will happily sit in a big pot or tub to decorate an area for years. Buy them as container-grown plants and simply transfer them at any time of year to your decorative pots. I once had a eucalyptus which began life growing in a tub for two years before taking up a permanent position in the garden. Hydrangeas take a lot of beating for a spot out of full sunlight; for early flower you can buy them as house plants and, when winter frosts are over, transplant them to outdoor containers.

Other first-rate subjects for very large pots and tubs are the green and gold evergreen Elaeagnus pungens maculata and the evergreen-foliaged elaeagnus ebbingei, which has a silver underside to its leaves. Skimmia and aucuba (spotted laurel) might also be considered. Grey foliage plants adapt extremely well to container life; senecio greyii (laxifolius), for example, if well cut back every March will make a delightful bush with golden daisy flowers in summer; it looks particularly well in terracotta. Variegated hollies, miniature conifers, will all give pleasure in a terrace pot. Try to mix and match their colours, shapes, and textures. Conifers. by the way, can be kept compact by pinching the new growths back.

Many climbers can be grown in a tub or big pot, and might be the answer to the problem of having no flower bed near a house wall. Tropaeolum canariense (Canary creeper), Thunbergia alata (black-eyed Susan), with white, yellow and orange flowers, often with a black eye, clematis, golden and variegated hops, vines, honeysuckle, sweet peas, passiflora (the passion

Things which smell nice are lovely to have close to the house, and containers planted with stock are magnificent. I specially favour Brompton stock, which make fine pot plants. I sow the seed in seed-boxes in spring and more in June, transplant the seedlings into pots, and finally into the big containers the following spring ready for flowering. In the north it is probably best to keep the young plants in a cold frame during winter, or better still the sunroom. Some, I find, go on to become an almost permanent feature in an outdoor container but eventually they grow woody-stemmed and straggly and must be replaced. Heliotrope, mignonette, and many more flowers can be raised from seed to enjoy at flower), which is generally sold in pots, and variegated ivies will all climb, but they will also trail if not staked and in a very tall container on a plinth this can be very striking indeed. If the growth gets too full and bushy, careful pruning will control it.

If you look around and observe what others are doing with containers you will see that the best effects are won where there is good contrast of shape, form, or colour, and where each container is in harmony with its surroundings. At Osborne House on the Isle of Wight, for example, bold scarlet no-nonsense geraniums are planted profusely in large stone urns, where they are seen as splendid plantings against a refreshing backdrop of the green well-tended lawns and the sea. Not everyone has the sea at the back door, but some of us have walls or balustrades so that a pot or urn can be placed high to be seen silhouetted against the sky.

When visiting stately homes watch out for good examples of such plantings. See, for example, the famous gardens at Sissinghurst Castle in Kent, where the garden writer Vita Sackville-West furnished many containers with flowers and her example is still followed. In the entrance courtyard there · are stone pots filled with hydrangeas, and a large enviable glazed Chinese butter jar in the White Garden dates from the third century B.C. It is simply planted up with ivies.

Enjoy studying the shapes of containers and, when arranging them outdoors, set rounds against rectangular shapes, tall slim pots against squat fat ones, and so on, so that the eye is delighted. A pot placed against a plain wall might stand in a mock alcove constructed from trellis. If

The beauty of any container is lost if it becomes shabby.

the wall were white the trellis might be painted soft grey, blue, or sage green, even a quite bright colour in some situations. In a small town garden a mirror can be fixed in the alcove to give the illusion of a larger garden. It rarely pays to try to copy slavishly something you have seen elsewhere; whatever inspires you will probably need to be adapted to your own situation – and in any case it is always more interesting to let your own imagination get to work.

5
CARING FOR A BASKET

As only a few pounds of compost, at most, can be accommodated in the average hanging basket, window box, or other container, and this will be the only support the plants will have, it is obviously sound practice to use good compost so that they grow away well right from the start. Too many people simply dig up a spadeful of any old earth from the garden, thinking that as so little is required it is hardly worth the bother and expense of buying a bag of special compost. This is a great mistake, and problems can result. Soil lifted from the garden is often impoverished or otherwise unsuitable. I recommend you buy a bag of John Innes Compost No. 2, to which I always add a few handfuls of peat to lighten it.

A hanging basket must be lined before being filled with compost. Green sphagnum moss, which has always traditionally been used for this purpose, can be gathered in woods in moist areas if you know where to look and can get permission from the landowner. Fortunately, Woolworth's and most florists sell it along with wire hanging baskets. Reindeer moss, a curly kind of moss, comes in big dried-out packs which have to be soaked before use. This moss has the advantage that it looks good even when it is not very moist. I have successfully used moss scraped up with a rake from a friend's lawn in springtime – and it is very satisfactory to put such a tiresome thing to such a good use.

Many people use black or green plastic film as a liner, but personally I think this is ugly when viewed from underneath. This is certainly true until the plants become established and hang down to cover the sides, or unless some of the planting is done through holes made in the sides. It really is far prettier to do the basket in the old way. I knew someone who lined a basket with moss and then interlined it with plastic, but this proved not very successful as the plastic prevented the moss receiving any moisture and it soon turned brown. Even so, I thought the dark matt brown moss looked far better than the shiny plastic.

I have heard of baskets being lined with hessian, sacking, and artificial 'grass' sold for patios. I prefer a suitable growing plant as a lining, and I have used many things, including low-growing mat-like alpines such as stonecrop. I have even used the moss which grows in 'pads' on a low garage roof at the back of my house. Really, I have found you can use any moss you can come by, though it should be reasonably thick, and the short velvety kinds must be in large pieces. If you can get only small pieces, line your basket first with fine mesh chickenwire. Truly the only moss I have found useless was some short stuff brought me by a friend from sandy woodland; it was impossible to handle without it breaking up. Most mosses stay nicely green if the basket is properly and regularly watered.

Best of all linings, to my mind, is Arenaria balearica, a charming little lime-green evergreen foliage plant studded in summer with tiny white stars. Normally a plant seen growing in crevices of walls and paving, it is beautiful all the year round and is like a specially lush green moss. If kept regularly watered it will never go brown. If you do not already have it in the garden you will need to buy a number of plants to line a basket. However, if you do have it handily growing, as I do, you can simply lift a 'mat' of it. Place it in the basket 'growing side out', of course. Used in an indoor hanging basket, for example in a sunroom, it grows quite fluffy and luxuriant and quite changes its character.

Among alpines I have used as basket liners, in addition to stonecrop, are asperula suberosa (like a pink-flowered stonecrop), dwarf campanulas, aubretia, dwarf alpine helichrysum (with grey or silver foliage). Also successful are violets, helxine (mind your own business), and for indoors nertera depressa (bead plant), a tiny creeping herb which covers itself with many little orange berries.

First cover the bottom of the basket thickly with moss or your chosen plant material (I sometimes mix several different ones for unusual effects) and bring the lining about two inches up the sides of the basket. At this stage many people place a plate or saucer in the bottom of the basket to help hold water. I don't do this myself, for it seems almost certain that any plants or moss under the plate will brown and die. However, if you wish to try it, a deep plastic saucer of the kind sold to go under plant pots serves well as a small reservoir of water in dry conditions.

Other people recommend an extra lining of turf, grass side out, or bulb fibre on top of the moss. I would not personally introduce grass to my baskets in this way, as in my experience it simply grows out through the moss towards the light, and I think most of us have enough trouble grass cutting on the lawn without having to clip grass round a hanging basket.

Line the basket with moss or similar plant material.

Above: Fill centre with compost. Below: Finished arrangement.

Container-grown plants for those without a real garden.

Water your hanging baskets by immersing them in a large bowlful of water for half an hour. You can speed up by watering the top of the basket with a can — above. Then place your basket over a bucket to drain — below.

Continue lining the basket with moss, bringing it up the sides and filling in with compost as you go. If you want trailing plants to grow out from the sides, plant these as you proceed, laying the plant on its side, covering the roots with compost, and firming it in so that you leave no pockets of air. Do not take the compost right up to the top, though the moss lining should reach the rim. After planting up to the top leave a small depression towards the centre of the surface of the compost, to hold water.

Some baskets, such as the white plastic-covered wire ones, are so attractive in their own right that I sometimes leave a couple of inches clear of lining and compost. This seems specially appealing when a basket is planted at the top with decorative foliage plants, or when the basket is hanging in a sun room or conservatory which has white furniture.

It is sometimes recommended that, before planting, a basket should be well watered and allowed to drain. I do not find this very practical, for the wet compost makes the job of planting messy and dirty. I plant first and then water the basket, and if the compost then compacts I just top up with a little more. John Innes Compost used straight out of the bag is, I find, usually moist enough to handle, but if it is very dry I add a little water from a can with a rose, spraying it straight into the bag and mixing it until the compost just holds together when squeezed lightly in the hand.

Planting at the top can consist of one vigorous trailing plant, placed in the centre, or four or five plants placed round the edges with one in the centre. I was talking to a member of a municipal parks department and was admiring a trailing variegated plectranthus in a hanging basket. I was told that they place one plant in each basket and in a season that cascading growth can reach as much as ten feet and has to be trimmed back. The idea is lovely for an indoor decoration, especially in a conservatory, covered walk, or on a balcony or verandah.

To get a really trim and rounded effect with any basket which contains a trailing plant, hairpins or short U-shaped pieces of wire can be used to hold the outward-growing stems close in to the sides of the basket. For more free or unrestricted growth, just let the plants go their own sweet way. The tailored-looking basket is easy to achieve if only neat-growing plants of one kind are chosen, instead of a mixture of plants of different habits,

Beautifully grown but a little dull — we've seen it all before.

which result in baskets of haphazard shape (though these have their own definite charm).

With such plants as fuchsia, geranium, lobelia, ivy, etc., four or five plants are required to fill the top of the average basket to provide a really good show. Obviously the earlier the planting is done, the better and longer-lasting display we shall have. Anyone who has a light, airy, frost-free place, such as a sunroom or conservatory, can plant up a basket in April and get a head start on those who have to wait for the end of the frosts, which can mean as late as the end of May in most parts of Britain. Using hardy plants, however, we

Poor man's orchid (schizanthus) cascading down.

where necessary for the plants to grow through. The idea is that the plastic conserves moisture. A covering of damp moss can serve the same purpose. The same idea can be adapted for troughs, window boxes, etc., especially where the top surface is above eye level. The edges may need to be held down with small stones, hair pins or can even be stapled down to a wooden container. Suitable plastic is sold in rolls but these are far too big for the average person with just one or two window boxes or baskets. In this case the answer is to cut up an ordinary black plastic dustbin liner.

The importance of watering

I have found that when making up a hanging basket of permanent subjects, such as ivy, it is a good plan to leave the basket standing on the ground in a shady place for a week or two after planting. This encourages good rooting to take place if the basket is watered carefully and saves the plants being rocked about in the wind while they are getting established.

On the subject of watering, I always try to make things as easy as possible for myself by positioning baskets at eye-level or at least within arm's reach, to avoid having to climb up on a stool or stepladder. Don't water in 'dribs and drabs' – do it thoroughly and regularly. A sad sight in winter is the basket which has been left hanging forlornly with its summer plants long dead. It is probably too high to have encouraged regular watering and attention. Once a basket has really dried out the plants will take ages to recover, if they ever do.

Undoubtedly baskets need a deep drink every week, perhaps twice or three times a week, or

can make up a basket at any time of year, except in snow or hard frost, and either put it outside or enjoy it indoors.

Potted plants should have been watered an hour or so before they are ready for final planting in the basket, so that they will knock out easily from their pots or boxes with a few sharp taps on the side. This also prevents the soil coming away from the roots. Make a hole in the compost to receive each plant, and press the compost firmly round the roots.

A round covering of black or green plastic film at the top of an exposed basket, or one which hangs high under a clear glass or plastic roof, can be an advantage. Suitably sized holes are made

even every day or twice a day in windy, dry, or sunny weather, or when hanging in exposed places. Thirsty baskets result, too, when they are sited in sheltered courtyards surrounded by walls which store up heat during summer days and continue to give it off hours after the sun has gone.

The best way to give a basket a deep drink is to use an old washing-up bowl filled with water (a liquid plant feed can be added occasionally). The bowl should be large enough for the basket to be immersed with room to spare for the side growths so that they do not get bruised or damaged. The water should reach almost to the top of the basket. The drinking process can be

speeded by watering the top of the basket with a can. Flowering side growths and trailing growths can be placed over the edge of the bowl so that they are never submerged. Contact with the water can spoil delicate 'thin' petals, and a soaking under water will make double flowers 'ball' – their petals stick together and they look a sorry sight. The roots, of course, revel in their bath. I give a soaking of about half an hour and then stand each basket gently on a bucket to drain well before re-hanging. This method does not work with a hanging container which has no drainage holes. In this case the soil should be tested for dryness with the fingers; the moment it feels dry just below the surface is the moment to water. One soon develops a 'feel' for this. A plant which is actually growing in the container can be watered with a can, but one which is in its own pot inside the container can be simply lifted out, pot and all, and immersed in a bowl of water.

A tier of wall baskets, one above another, reduces the daily watering chore – water the top one with your can and the surplus will run down on to the one below, and so on. However, all the baskets should be taken down regularly for a really good soak in a bucket or bowl. At all times keep a can of water handy to nudge your memory about watering. Rainwater is generally preferable to tap water if you can collect enough in a butt or buckets and bowls.

Some plants, such as button daisies, pansies, and fuchsias, have little built-in resistance to drought. If they are allowed to dry out and flag they can rarely be completely brought back to full health. A first-aid treatment for flagging plants is to completely immerse them in water for a couple of hours. When the basket is returned to its hook, a large plastic bag is pulled right over it, plants and all. Make as good a closure as you can and leave this mini-greenhouse overnight. More often than not, every plant will be crisp and well by morning – and we can resolve never to let them dry out again!

With constant regular watering the top surface of compost in a basket exposed to sun or wind may soon form a crust through which water may then find difficulty in penetrating. The remedy is gently to stir up the surface compost; weeding also helps. In the growing season all plants in hanging baskets should be fed one of the proprietary liquid feeds once a week (though I know people who swear by cold tea!) Do not feed sick plants, one which is resting after flowering, or the newly planted. A feed just before flowering is most helpful. Liquinure, Maxicrop, Kerigrow, and Baby Bio are among the many available. Baskets outdoors usually need feeding every week from around mid-June until first frosts.

6
HOW DOES YOUR CONTAINER GROW?

Boxes, tubs, and similar containers for planting should if possible have a number of drainage holes in the bottom. Each hole is carefully covered with a piece of broken flower pot (crock) and then the whole of the base is covered with about an inch deep of small stones or crocks. Over this place a layer of turf, coarse moss, peat, or dead leaves. Then fill up with John Innes Compost No. 2.

Take the compost to about an inch below the rim – many people make the mistake of filling right to the top, which makes watering difficult. A suitable tray containing a layer of pebbles, placed under the box, is a help to drainage. Some

Assemble materials.

Clear drain holes.

Line container with broken flower pot crocks.

Add compost and prepare holes for plants.

Remove plants from pots and position in container.

Your finished arrangement should have this informal look.

experts suggest leaving the container for a week for the compost to settle before planting. I think that is unrealistic; the majority of people – including me – can't wait to put the plants in at once!

When planting, remember that an informal effect is better than a regimented one which results from placing plants in rows. Obviously tall plants need to be at the back or sides, and shorter or trailing ones at the front and sometimes the sides. I find it useful to arrange the plants experimentally before removing them from their individual pots. By standing back and walking around I can achieve an appearance which is balanced and effective both from indoors and out. After planting I like to give the container a top covering of peat, pebbles, Forest Bark, or small stones to act as a mulch and prevent too much evaporation; this treatment gives a smart, neat finish to the container at the same time. Now give the planting a really good watering with a can which has a fine rose. Take the water right over the foliage to freshen it and wash away any soil which may be adhering. Do this in shade, for the sun's rays on wet leaves may damage them.

As I have said, I like to .have a number of containers coming along as seasonal replacements to bring into prominent positions when others finish flowering. An alternative is to fill permanent containers with compost, Forest Bark, or peat and use this simply as a means of supporting plants in pots, which can be replaced as and when necessary. If the whole thing is kept watered and the plants given an occasional feed you will find they romp away in the idyllic conditions of constant humidity coming up around them from the compost. Indeed, more often than not when the pots are removed the plants will be found to have rooted out through the hole in the bottom of the pot and into the compost.

Regular removal of dead flowerheads before a plant can set its seed is important for a long flowering season in all containers, and I always do this job at the same time as watering. Dead, dying, or insect-nibbled foliage should also be removed, as should any dead wood. Boxes containing bulbs which have finished flowering are best moved out of public view until the foliage dies down; it is important to leave the foliage on, as it feeds up the bulb for the following year.

Perennials should be cut back, and divided if necessary, in the autumn. Geraniums and fuchsias should be either moved in their containers to a light, airy, and frost-free place before the frosts come, or else lifted and replanted in suitable pots, but if you do not have room indoors for a number of large plants you can gently prune back the roots and cut back the plants. In late winter or early spring new growth will quickly get under way. By feeding all winter, a geranium will probably flower all winter indoors.

Daisies in spring, petunias all summer/autumn; euonymus in winter.

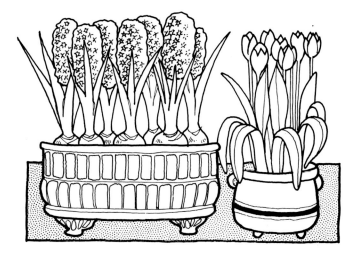

A pot of trailing lobelia well suits its cottage surroundings.

I put most of my indoor baskets, boxes, etc. out of doors when there is any light, warm rain in spring, summer, or autumn. This is a marvellous wash and pick-me-up. I even put out collections which are growing together, and single plants which have no drainage holes in their containers. It generally takes rain some time to penetrate any depth, and by then I will have brought them in again. If it rains so hard that a plant is standing in a puddle of water, which really is too much, I simply lay the container on its side to drain for an hour or two. The only disadvantage of this whole system (or perhaps I should say advantage) is that it usually stops raining as soon as I have taken everything outside!

Many writers warn against the danger of over-watering plants growing in containers. This frightens many inexperienced people into erring so far in the other direction that their plants die of dehydration, or take so long to recover from the enforced thirst that they never make more than puny specimens with a half-starved look. With experience you get the feel of the thing, learning the signs a plant gives to let us know when it is dying for a drink, such as lightly flagging foliage and drooping flowers. The soil or compost feels dry to the touch; when you tap a pot it rings rather than gives off a dull sound. Dig your finger into the compost just under the surface to test how dry or damp it is – this is my favourite method. When a little water is poured on, very dry earth or compost will make a soft crackling sound which you can hear if you listen carefully, and this is a very good indication that watering is required.

Plants need a great deal of water when they are growing well, and in warm conditions. Watering everything perhaps once a week is not a good system, for the requirements of each plant differ according to the time of the year, its state of growth, and so on. Watering large containers can be a problem in spells when the earth has really dried out and water poured on the surface tends to run straight off. One solution is to sink one or more pieces of pipe or tubing vertically into the soil, or use a slim plastic bottle, with the bottom cut away, in the same manner. Water is poured down the tubes or into the bottle, and so penetrates to where it is needed, at root level. The device can usually be disguised with bits of moss, pebbles, or something similar, if the plants are not sufficiently big to cover it from view. There are also many useful automatic watering systems on sale, ideal when plants under cover of balconies etc. have to be left during holidays and other absences from home.

When the weather is warm and dry an overhead spraying is appreciated by most plants, particularly on their foliage, for it creates humidity as well as removing dust, freshening the colours, and generally livening everything up. It is amazing how dirty plants can get outdoors, in particular if they are near a drive or the road. I sometimes use an ordinary watering can with the rose in place, as this provides both a spray and an ordinary watering at the same time, but more effective is a small mist spray which can be held in one hand. The spray is fine enough to be directed exactly where you want it. Spraying also discourages that scourge of plants in dry sheltered places, the red spider. If you find that flowers have flagged very badly, perhaps on a very warm day, first water them well (even if the sun is beating down) then cover the whole container flowers and all with a double sheet of damp newspaper. Cover the newspaper with a sheet of lightweight polythene, which prevents the damp paper drying out. This treatment provides the plants with a moist atmosphere to revive them, and also keeps off the worst of the sun. Remove the polythene and newspaper in the cool of the evening or the following morning.

Lots of indoor container plants find it a bit of a treat to be put outside for a 'summer holiday', after the risk of late frosts is past. Round about early June I put many of my indoor plants out into window boxes, tubs, baskets, or other containers. Indoor plants can be planted directly into the containers or else plunged into large

Double petunias in this old china bowl look delightful.

containers still in their own pots, the space between being filled with gravel. I find they usually thrive and make a good show. Colours and leaf patterns become brighter and livelier, and the plants will often burst into bloom for the first time. In fact, they seem to generally enjoy themselves. This can certainly be a tonic for a slightly ailing plant. If possible, select a sheltered, warm, slightly shady position for it. Make a daily check on plants in outdoor containers for watering and signs of greenfly and other pests.

Indoor plants which I have found greatly benefit from a refreshing spell outside during the summer months are all kinds of geraniums (pelargoniums), bilbergia, ferns (placed in a very shady

A blue cutlery drainer is pressed into service!

border), ivies, the kangaroo vine (cissus), aspidistra, pittosporum, grape ivy (Rhoicissus rhomboidea), mother-of-thousands (Saxifraga stolonifera, or S. sarmentosa), streptocarpus – a broken leaf will root in a shady border, campanula isophylla, plectranthus, pilea, fatshedera, aphelandra, aechmea, and Dracaena marginata tricolor. Keep an eye on them, and if they show the slightest sign of discomfort bring them indoors again.

Shelter from wind

One of the main problems in caring for outdoor container plants is the effect of the wind, particularly with window boxes and containers on open balconies, as in a block of flats. Sometimes a shelter can be arranged with glass or transparent plastic panels, or trellis. The latter will provide excellent support for a winter jasmine, clematis, a summer rose, a vine, or a berrying cotoneaster, planted in a big tub or box. Such subjects give a country garden look, as well as helping to filter the wind. In late spring a windbreak of striped canvas or similar material can be fixed round the railings of a balcony or outside landing.

Containers in a high position dry out tremendously quickly, and special attention must be paid to watering, even in wet weather, for eaves and projecting balconies keep off a surprising amount of rain. Always choose the largest containers that can safely be accommodated, for the more compost they hold the less quickly they will dry out. Liberal top dressings of moisture-holding peat or leaf mould will help protect against drought.

In positions where watering really is difficult, choose plants which actually relish a dry root run. Succulents are often beautiful and make fine plants which colour well; a box of mixed kinds can look fantastic. But there are many other plants which stand up to exposure to sun and periods of drought. These include all the achilleas, sempervivums and sedums, agapanthus, gypsophila (including the dwarf varieties), dimorphotheca hybrids (daisy-like colourful flowers from South Africa), nepeta (catmint), lychnis flos Jovis (pretty pink campion), helianthemum (sun rose), and bergenia. There are also nasturtium, arabis, armeria (thrift), mesembryanthemum (Livingstone daisy), and many grey-leaved plants such as artemisias and Senecio greyii (laxifolius), which I cut back hard in March to keep them small and bushy. You can grow all the yuccas well in appalling conditions of drought, and none flags or sulks. If you are away a lot, avoid subjects which need regular attention, such as fuchsias and begonias, unless you have self-watering containers or a very good neighbour who will take over.

I personally detest staked plants in containers; I tend to think that if stakes have to be used the wrong plant has been chosen in the first place. You may not agree with this. Container gardening is highly individual, and there is nothing to prevent your growing long-stemmed tulips and daffodils in windy window boxes complete with stakes or bits of bushy twigs to support them. But do try to keep the supports as unobtrusive as possible, like a friend of mine who uses old steel knitting needles painted green, with knitting wool for ties. If I do have to tie up climbers or other floppy plants I prefer soft plastic ties to wire. A packet of darning wool goes a long way, and as this is not usually pure wool nowadays it does not shrink and grip the stems too tightly. Bass or garden string is also good. Make a loop first round the stake, then lightly round the plant stem, then back round the stake and tie off.

Many plants, such as ordinary snapdragons, pelargoniums, and wallflowers make shorter and bushier plants, well filled with side shoots which flower profusely – ideal for container gardening – if the growing tips are pinched out when the plants are still quite young. This may seem like folly to the new gardener. In fact, it coaxes shoots which would otherwise remain dormant to break

Two containers nicely staged to display these succulents.

into growth. If, as sometimes occurs, one side shoot then grows away strongly, while others seem not to progress so well, pinch out the tip of the strong shoot once more. In these ways a sturdy and well-shaped plant results.

Anyone who has no frost-free place in which to keep them for the winter must sacrifice all tender-growing subjects at the end of the season. Otherwise, keep them free of frost and bring them into growth again in the early part of the year. Tuberous begonias and dahlias should be lifted, dried off at the end of the season, and stored carefully indoors until setting them to shoot beside a window in March.

Some so-called annuals can be overwintered if kept out of frost, and I have brought lobelia and petunias safely through the winter in my glazed porch. Frost strikes free-standing objects from all sides, so if no other protection can be arranged in the very hardest weather it is wise to move any containers holding plants which might be vulnerable, such as 'hardy' fuchsias, into the shelter provided by the angle of two walls, a porch, or cover them with branches from an evergreen.

In the spring I often re-stock containers such as window boxes with plants lifted from a border and just coming into flower. They 'get away' more quickly than their fellows left behind in the border, quickly opening buds and displaying themselves like prima donnas. This may be because of the extra shelter afforded by the house walls. Similarly, containers sometimes seem to suit some plants better than direct planting in the garden. To give an example, forget-me-nots which normally quickly look pale and washed-out during wet spells retain good colour when planted in window boxes etc. because of the good drainage and the fact that they can dry out the moment the rain eases.

I always try to position my outdoor containers with care as to the chosen plant's requirements. Take cacti and succulents – they do best when kept rather on the dry side and will not appreciate a damp, shady situation in the garden. Placing them in shallow pans and bowls suits them and makes an attractive display, particularly in a situation such as on either side of a short flight of steps.

Container plants need feeding, in the same way as those grown in hanging baskets. Use any of the well-known brands of liquid or foliar feed. If any fertiliser other than a liquid is used it is necessary to water the plants before and after applying.

After the end of the first year it pays to replace the compost in window boxes and other containers, including baskets. Where permanent plantings of shrubs, perennials, etc., have been made, take out as much compost as possible without disturbing the roots, and replace carefully with fresh compost which has had a little bonemeal stirred into it.

7

BE WISE COLOUR-WISE

We are all individuals and we choose the colours of paintwork, curtains, sunblinds and so on because *we* like them. We can continue these colours when choosing plants and flowers. It is a good idea when planning hanging baskets, window boxes, and other containers for plants to mentally step right outside the very familiarity of the house and try to see it as others might.

A colourful hanging basket or window box can even be used to disguise an unattractive view from inside the house as well as looking good from the street. If the only thing you can see from the window is a brick wall opposite, try to think of it as a backdrop to your planting. Use it, play it up, work it into your scheme by choosing colours which complement it or contrast with it.

A cool grey wall opposite will make tomato-red begonias stand out in exciting contrast, while pink and blue flowers will be enchanting, and clear yellow African or French marigolds will practically sing. If you face an orange-red brick wall, choose just the right shade of apricot, lime-green, brown, plum, or grey − all these colours can be found in plants, especially those grown principally for their foliage.

Similarly, a brightly-planted container in your own garden will draw the eye away from the central heating oil tank or next door's garden shed. To be really successful, colour plantings in window boxes and other containers must be

carefully considered together with the character of the house and the materials from which it is built. We have probably all noticed how a flowering pink cherry blossoming in springtime looks superb when seen against a blue sky and 'nothing' against an orange-red brick building. If we take care over such details we can achieve splendid planned-looking effects with no more effort, no more cost, than for a scheme which blends poorly. Yet it is surprising how often this is forgotten or ignored.

And walls can be painted, or even bits of them. Fresh white walls show off all colours excellently, and the green of foliage looks smart against white. However, white must be kept sparkling

white. Wall paints for outdoors are available also in many other colours nowadays.

Whether planting up hanging baskets, window boxes, or tubs first-rate visual impact is achieved by keeping the colours sharp, clean cut, and definite, and choosing plants with not too greatly varied a colour mix. Having said that, it must be admitted that in some situations a multi-coloured planting can be a real crowd-stopper. It is largely a matter of playing it by eye and then learning from experience.

I greatly admired a colour scheme I saw recently. Three big boxes arranged on one side of the entrance steps to a stylish town house brilliantly led the eye up from pavement level to the front door. All the planting was kept to low carpets of massed pansies. The lowest box had deep purple flowers, the middle one had gold, and the top one had cream. Few of us would have the courage to stick to just one flower type and use it in such solid blocks of colour.

A friend of mine has a field opposite her cottage; in summer it is sunny with buttercups. She too fills her window boxes with pansies, of the same colour as the buttercups, and the effect when seen from inside the sitting room, which has soft green watered silk curtains and primrose-yellow cushion covers, is striking. Thus can really wonderful colour effects be won very simply at the cost of a little time, imagination, and enthusiasm.

Window box and other container plantings can be arranged to colour-match the plants growing near them out of doors. I remember seeing a stone building with a rather severe forecourt which had been enlivened with tubs in which hellebores hung jade-green bells against the stones, lime-yellow euphorbia lit up a dark corner, and a golden ivy cavorted up a wall so that the eye was irresistibly drawn to window boxes emblazoned with polyanthus in orange, yellow, and gold.

White hanging baskets and white boxes on a stone window ledge can look marvellous planted up with pale pinks and reds to complement richer pink roses growing nearby. Blue hydrangeas and white agapanthus in containers can be colour-linked with a blue ceanothus climbing up a white trellis. A striped garden awning might well be in hot bright colours and for summer days one of these colours could be repeated in the planting scheme. And why not, if you liked the colours well enough to buy the awning? A hundred years ago Victorian gardeners were using scarlet geraniums, trailing blue lobelia, and purple petunias in their hanging baskets, and the habit is still with us. Yet many other colours are possible in even the simplest scheme, and this is an age when most people take far more interest in colour around the home.

'Can I plant some red Busy Lizzies in my hanging basket?' someone asked me the other day. Well, there's no law against it! If 'doing your own thing' about colour will not stick out like a sore thumb in your neighbourhood, why not paint your front door some jewel-bright colour and put up eye-catching window boxes and hanging baskets planted to match? With such a bold scheme, though, it must be a point of honour to keep everything in good order.

A clear plain colour is best for containers as a rule, though last year I enjoyed seeing window boxes, outside a small mews house, painted vivid sea-blue. Each box was decorated on the front

with a white cut-out daisy. The boxes, a hanging basket, and two tubs either side of the garage door were filled to overflowing with marguerites.

Overall colour schemes

Round a square or close, or along a short street, or in a block of flats it would be nice if occasionally all the householders could get together to produce some overall colour scheme for their window boxes or other plantings. For individualists, however, there are plenty of ideas to be found. I recently admired a large cartwheel painted in a colour to match the house and hung around with potted plants.

Another idea I liked, outside a 'gipsy' caravan, was an arrangement of three gaily-painted barge water cans planted up with coleus plants which complemented the strong colours and patterns on the cans. Both these novel ideas fitted the homes which they adorned, for at all times everything must marry together easily, so that people say 'Gosh, how clever' rather than 'Heavens, what a sight!'

What about making a leafy jungle around the front door with wall-hung boxes and individual pots? These might be placed on wooden shelving painted to match the door. Another way would be to place wall baskets and tubs around a piece of sculpture – wood, stone, or ceramic. This can look fine arranged against a plain white wall, and here sculptural foliage will really come into its own. There are inexpensive yet good-looking lion masks and cherub heads on sale, meant actually as water spouts for garden pools, and they make excellent wall pieces to give emphasis to a grouping of plant containers.

Colour and texture can be exploited in all kinds of interesting ways. For instance, a stone birdbath might make a very unusual container for 'grow anywhere' plants, like bright yellow stonecrop or mixed houseleeks with their subtle colouration, even if the birdbath has no drainage hole. I make a mound of compost rather than leaving it level below the rim of the bath. Climb pastel-coloured sweet peas and yellow canary creeper or variegated ivies up a metal or wickerwork bedhead fastened to a wall, to make a dramatic feature for, say, the balcony of a flat. These bedheads with their swirling designs make remarkably handsome and original supports for climbing plants.

In some situations a large, deep, home-made wooden box lacquered a brilliant Chinese red or orange can look expensively effective with, for example, flamboyantly-coloured nasturtiums growing out of it, or try yellow and orange Charm or Cascade chrysanthemums. This scheme might not look so good in the depths of the country against old timbers (where the box might be better stained to link with its surroundings) but could be stunning outside a smart town dwelling. Novel ideas soon come with a little imagination. How about hanging an old birdcage, painted gold, in the entrance to a town garden? Plant it with variegated ivies, ferns, or fuchsias. It can hang from its own stand, or from a simple archway of white, blue, or green trellis. Tomato plants are a good crop to grow on a patio but they do not look noticeably attractive. So paint a long broom handle white and pin coloured plastic ribbon around it, like a barber's pole. A tripod or 'wigwam' of such poles also looks bright and effective as a support for runner beans or peas.

Near the sea I have seen old small boats used to great effect as planters, hung – not too high – from a handy beam by chains fore and aft. One I saw painted blue and white and planted with scarlet zinnias looked patriotic as well as eye-catching, but a totally different visual effect could be managed by planting with mixed jewel-coloured dwarf zinnias.

Ideas which might look funny in one situation are perfectly at home in another. Old oil drums may not immediately catch the imagination as containers, but I once saw them used to great effect as the entire container garden on the deck of a houseboat moored on the Thames in London. The boat itself was painted black and white, and the oil drums were black to match; they had been cut down to a variety of sizes and vigorously planted with flowers in a motley collection of colours.

On a smaller scale, the right corner can be happily brightened by hanging up one or more of those cutlery draining baskets in bright plastic and planting them with orange begonias or tagetes, or even (near the kitchen door, perhaps) parsley, chives, or mint. The young in heart might equally enjoy hanging a pillar-box red colander from scarlet cords and planting it with dwarf nasturtiums. Ideas like these are easy to think up and though they may seem gimmicky are usually fun – and inexpensive.

Do your own thing and be inventive, as much with colour as with the things you can press into service as plant containers. There is no special virtue in the British love of mixing lots of different plants (and colours) in one container.

Superb begonias used to add colour to a plain wall.

More memorable results may come for you by displaying a greater quantity of just one kind of plant in one container. You might experiment with mixed pink and white trailing geraniums (pelargoniums) or the hardy garden anthemis cupaniana with its grey foliage which is sprigged from early summer onwards with white daisies. After anthemis seem to have finished flowering you can cut back all the shoots which have bloomed and new shoots will continue to flower for many weeks.

Instead of one kind of plant in one container, what about that idea of just one colour? Variation and visual interest can still be achieved with variety of shape and texture, for one *colour*

need not necessarily mean only one kind of flower. You could have a refreshing scheme of frilly white azaleas under-planted with crisp white pansies in your window boxes, white trails of lobelia set off by more white pansies, or white begonias, in the hanging baskets, and white pelargoniums massed in boxes by the front porch. The flowers' own green foliage does, of course, make a cool setting for immaculate white.

Or one could go to the other extreme and select a more vivid colour, say joyous orange. There might be African marigolds of a good, strong, look-at-me orange, with pendulous tangerine begonias for the hanging baskets and paler orange tagetes in window boxes, and terracotta garden tubs might have gazanias with orange marigolds. Such colour schemes look magnificent if planted fearlessly, full and fairly close.

Another idea would be to take one colour, perhaps yellow, and ring changes on the theme with tints and shades ranging from pale creamy yellow to bright butter yellow, and even on towards copper or old gold. The flowers could be polyanthus, wallflowers, alyssum, and doronicum, with trailers of Hedera Goldheart or Hedera Buttercup for the spring.

Softly-coloured blue hydrangeas in tubs and boxes in summer could be colour-matched with hanging baskets of the ever-useful lobelia in pale to deep blues, both dwarf sorts and trailers, plus that remarkable nautical blue convolvulus tricolor 'Royal Ensign' to make the whole thing shipshape. The colours we use must depend on the plants we can get. Excellent sources are well-stocked nurseries and garden centres, Women's Institute market stalls, or florists' shops with good suppliers. Some of these, if we inquire early enough, will try to get the particular plants and colours we need. Other plants can be lifted from the garden as they come into flower, or can be specially grown in the garden in pots and transferred to the containers as they bud up. It is a matter of planning ahead, and it is best to try to resist the 'one of this and two of that' philosophy, the job lot of bulbs, and so forth, when you are hoping for a good display.

'Secret' containers

To be a constant joy and interest, not all containers need bold or startling colour schemes that can be seen from far away down the road. Some of my nicest and most memorable effects have been quieter, more subtle, and the more 'secret' boxes seen only from close at hand in the garden can often be the best-loved. All-foliage containers, without flowers, often come into this category, and I have a very great fondness for a couple of quiet little terracotta urns, and a matching hanging basket, planted up with echeveria which have delighted me all summer with their silver-blue colouring. And a small north-facing conservatory I painted white and once hung with baskets dripping with cool maidenhair ferns also proved memorable. These latter grew so well in the cool and moist conditions that they shed spores into boxes of other ferns below, and the resulting hundreds of baby maidenhair plants enabled me to give many to a plant stall at a charity fete. It is always an added pleasure when things do really well.

Gentle colours often create a perfect backcloth for brighter ones. Permanent plantings can make the soft colours, with annuals for the bright

Two or more pots make a feature in themselves.

accents in front. Hebe pagei (a form of shrubby veronica) is a charming little grey-blue carpeter which makes a dense cover in a container, and Hebe armstrongii is another dwarf veronica with an unusual old gold conifer-like effect. Skimmias, with good evergreen leaves and red berries, can all be used as settings for plants such as wallflowers, polyanthus, daffodils, in spring, and pansies, begonias, in summer. Another good shrub for large boxes is the variegated griselinia with its clean glossy leaves of yellow and green (so easy to grow from cuttings, which can be used in the larger boxes as they grow up).

A rather more everyday shrub is privet, which in its gold and variegated forms makes an

As here, the container should not detract from its contents.

simply with white flowers and green foliage. Or what about adding yellow, pink, or blue flowers to white ones in a white container, against the background of a wall or woodwork in brown, sage green, or even white – for even with white-against-white you get shadows and subtle differences of tone. I think that if a white container is used a touch of white should always be included in the plantings. Oddly enough, cream, once so popular and which blends nicely with many house colour schemes, is 'out' for containers at the moment with the commercial manufacturers, which seems a pity. However, if cream fits your scheme best there is nothing to prevent you painting your containers.

All the warm terracotta plant-pot colours must be used with some discretion. They show off sugary blue-pinks poorly, and are better with salmon pink, orange-red, lime green, silver-grey, pale lemon yellow, or ice blue, and ghastly with lavender or purple. On the other hand, stone-coloured containers display almost everything to advantage, making all colours look good.

Unless a planter is either antique or really beautiful in its own right I would never hesitate to colour it to go with the colour scheme I have in mind. If you really do not care for terracotta, for example, because it makes you think of ordinary plant pots, but you happen to like the shape of a particular terracotta planter, then paint it with a matt colour wash – house wall paint will do the job. I may change a pot's colour each season, to suit some new planting, and I don't mind painting a pot while the flowers are actually blooming if I find the overall colour effect is poor! So be brave. Go ahead with confidence – and change anything which doesn't work first time.

appealing plant for a container if kept clipped hard back – the golden ones always look as though the sun is shining on them. All the above make good foils, and hardy border plants which can be lifted from the garden and used in boxes and baskets for the same purpose include alchemilla mollis (lady's mantle), with its charming green foliage and showers of lime-green frothy flowers, all the hostas, which have firm sculptured leaves, and heuchera, an evergreen with pretty scalloped leaves.

Few people, in my experience, pay enough attention to the colour of containers when selecting the plants to go in them. White containers are popular and can look superb filled

Here are a few ideas for colour schemes:

Against red brick: Cool colours such as pale yellow, soft blue, cream, silver, lime green, white, orange-red.

With stone and concrete: All colours, but particularly apricot, coral, tangerine, all the blues from baby blue to navy, lilac, violet, citron yellow, rose pink, scarlet.

Colour-washed walls: Against soft blue walls, deep blue, fuchsia pink, Venetian red, grey, peach, orange, tan, clear primrose, brown, green; against white walls, almost all colours, but try to link plant and flower colours with any adjacent woodwork; against brown walls, white, pink, orange, pale blue, crisp yellows; against pale green walls, almost all colours, but try pink, deep cyclamen, plum, yellow, tan, brown, fiery reds, pale orange; against pale pink walls, old rose, green, white, brown, lilac, violet, spring greens.

8

SOMETHING FOR THE POT

To grow something delicious to eat if you have no garden or only a minute one may seem a bit of a pipe-dream. But with container gardening it is surprising how many fruits, vegetables, and herbs can be grown. They not only give crops but look interesting at the same time. You can even grow 'baked beans', the 12-inch-tall bean plants called Pearly King to serve with tomato sauce!

And what could look more appealing than a smart row of crisp green lettuce in the box outside the kitchen window? They could be interspersed with chives and parsley for variation of leaf, or with Swiss ruby chard which is edible, has attractive green leaves and plum-pink stems, and is decorative all winter if you don't eat it. Chives have an added bonus – purple mop-headed flowers. Even a radish has a neat leaf rosette, and could be sown along with ornamental cabbages or red, pink, white, and green decorative kale.

Here are some edible possibilities, depending on the size and depth of your window box or other suitable container:

Lettuce springs immediately to mind. It can be raised so easily from seed, which germinates readily out of doors or in the kitchen window. Sow the seed sparingly about $\frac{1}{2}$ an inch deep. A first sowing can be made on a mild day in March. The butterhead or crisphead lettuces are more

attractive visually than the cos, and can even make a pleasing accompaniment to a few scarlet geranium plants or dwarf African marigolds if you don't mind mixing the edible and inedible. Seedsmen's catalogues list a wide variety of lettuce, including one called Windowsill. Webb's Wonderful is a favourite, with its close-packed centre giving it a Peter Rabbit look. Tom Thumb is also good for our purpose, and what about a red-foliaged lettuce such as Red Grenoble, adding colour not only to the planting but to salads?

With a sheltered window box or patio planter tucked out of sight you could do as a flat-dwelling friend of mine does and put plastic cloches right over the containers, sowing in autumn Arctic King lettuce for early spring salad crops. There are also small plastic domes on sale under which lettuce will survive the winter. Lettuce does not like to dry out, and is best kept out of hot situations. Regular watering is very necessary or your lettuce will be inclined to run to seed – though this can be quite pretty to look at.

If you like garlic in cooking, buy a couple of bulbs, split off the individual cloves as though you were going to cook with them, and plant them in February. They like a light soil, and the cloves should be just covered with soil when planted. Water and feed regularly and lift the crop when the leaves die down in late summer, hanging the bulbs up to dry in the sunshine. A few cloves planted in the autumn in a sheltered box will supply fresh garlic early the following year. The foliage of garlic is onion-like and not particularly handsome, except that it gives a long-pointed leaf shape to a window box.

Strawberry plants give a touch of luxury to a window box or hanging basket in a sunny aspect, though they will not tolerate a dry, 'mean' soil. I have had great success with them in deep, rich loam which has been well manured, and with copious watering – really good soakings – particularly in dry weather, and regular liquid feeds. If strawberry plants are allowed to dry out the fruit shrivels, the plant looks sad, and possibly will not fruit again that year.

I find that a deep, average-sized hanging basket will support only two plants at the most, and needs constant attention. Deep window boxes and tubs are probably easier, and there are large strawberry pots which look elegant standing in tall windows. However, the little alpine strawberries are suitable for shallower containers, and look very pretty trailing their doll's house size fruits. Where some protection is available – for instance, in a conservatory or sun lounge – one can get a special strawberry growing kit. Tubes of polythene are hung vertically, filled with the growing medium provided. With the kit comes a sachet of plant nutrient, a trickle irrigation system, and a dozen strawberry plants. They are planted in July through holes made in the tubes. The whole thing is interesting, decorative, and takes up hardly any space.

Alpine strawberries are grown from seed in the early part of the year and fruit within three months of sowing. The small sweet fruits, usually sold only in the most exclusive shops, are really rather special. With all strawberries, take off the runners on sight the first year; in subsequent years runners can be allowed to grow on to make a new plant and so increasing the stock, for strawberry plants need to be replaced every three years. Buy virus-free plants rather than taking

Container-grown plants can offer more than decorative display. Many kinds of vegetables and fruits can be cultivated successfully in this way.

gifts from a friend, for these may have become diseased.

An enthusiast will never be defeated. A friend of mine who has only a tiny garden grows magnificent strawberries overhead by using an old length of roof guttering lined with polythene. It has holes in the bottom for drainage. The strawberries hang down clean and free of snail-bites and look superb.

Outdoor tomatoes have really come into their own with the advent of the special plastic bags full of compost or other growing medium, marketed under various names including Gro-bag and Growing Bag, into which the tomatoes are planted through holes cut in the top. Feeding is begun as the first truss of flowers begins to set fruit, using special liquid tomato feeds. The amount of watering required depends on the weather and the size of the plants, though the compost must always be kept thoroughly moist and an astonishing one-and-a-half gallons of water per bag per day may be required in very hot weather. This crop needs a sunny, sheltered position to succeed.

Dwarf tomatoes such as the two-foot-high Pixie could be planted either side of a deep window box. A friend of mine who always grows them gets an early and plentiful crop, even in a poor summer. One seedsman says that Pixie is the fastest-ripening tomato in the world. At any rate, it can be grown not only in outside window boxes, pots, planters, etc but also as an attractive indoor cropper for winter if a few plants are raised in late summer.

Tiny Tim is a 15-inch-high baby which gives many bright scarlet small fruits. There is even a tomato offered specially for hanging baskets, as well as window boxes etc. It is called Sub Arctic Cherry; it makes a low, spreading, pendulous growth. Other useful kinds include Primabel, Roma, and the F.1 hybrid Sigmabush; all do well outdoors. For something unusual there are tomatoes with yellow and red stripes – Mr. Stripy and Tigerella – and the gold-fruited Golden Sunrise. Or you could try a packet of Mixed Ornamental, which produces a mixture of miniature fruits, red and yellow and pear, plum, and currant shaped, for use in salads and hors d'oeuvres. Sow the seed from January to March in heat, such as a warm kitchen. Prick out into pots and plant outdoors no earlier than late May to June.

Your own peppers

The same plastic cultivation bags can also be used to grow peppers, aubergines, and courgettes. One firm supplied schools in Southwark with miniature bags and this was so successful that the firm also supplied residents in a block of flats in London's dockland with full-sized bags, plants to grow in them, and instructions on cultivation. The balconies soon became bowers of fruiting and flowering plants and the crops of tomatoes, courgettes, etc., delighted the residents who could otherwise not have 'gardened'.

Peppers, to be successful out of doors, need a very sunny and sheltered position. You can grow them from seed or buy in young plants. The latter have been quite easy to obtain during the last few years, though as always the advantages of raising your own from seed include being able to choose which variety to grow. There are such exotics as Slim Pim, which crops heartily out of doors,

Culinary herbs grouped with pansies in an old sink, near the kitchen door, is both practical and pretty.

Again in a sunny spot or window, you can grow aubergines. The flowers are most decorative, even if you do not succeed in cropping any fruit, being purple with a yellow eye.

Scarlet runner beans, sometimes called climbing stick beans, are equally attractive in flower as well as producing a very worthwhile crop. I have grown them successfully not only in deep boxes but as a lovely jungly trailing plant in a large white plastic bucket hanging from a roof beam on a balcony. They need a good rich compost and regular feeding and watering, and as with many other fruiting subjects a light spray over the flowers with plain water each day helps the fruit to set. Sow the seed March–April, 2 inches deep and 6 inches apart. Support the young growth with twiggy sticks such as snippings of dead privet, or you can grow them up trellis – I have actually seen them grown round a front door, where they gave a long period of colour – plus, of course, a crop of beans.

Even a garage wall could be used for beans, with the plants trained up wires, plastic mesh, or what you will. Although the familiar red flowers are very pretty there are other runner beans with white or orange flowers which might well fit in better with your own colour scheme. The beans are just as succulent. There are also beans with gold and purple pods; and dwarf and bush beans for a low-growing crop. Planting dwarf French marigolds between the beans is said to keep away greenfly and blackfly.

Variegated flower cabbage is a super plant for window boxes, patio planters, even hanging baskets, out of doors, for it is at its most colourful, providing crisp decorative rosettes of pink, lavender, purple, white, and green, in the cold

giving fruits of about 2½ inches long for casseroles, salads, etc; Canape Hybrid, the recognisably supermarket sort; and Pedro, a tomato-shaped pepper for a very warm wall or inside a sunroom window. The peppers come dark green, turning red later. Pick them before they reach too large a size, thus encouraging the plants to produce more fruit. Some people prune them right back and grow them on indoors for a second year's harvest.

months of winter. Indeed, it colours best of all in the frostiest weather. To eat it would be a sin! It is a 'must' for winter decoration, and the decorative kales can look equally attractive; one called Strawberries and Cream looks as delicious as its name. Kales and flower cabbages are grown from seed sown in spring and planted out as they begin to make sizeable plants.

Seakale beet (Swiss ruby chard) is such a handsome sea beet which, even if you could not eat it, would still be worth a place in anyone's window box and is quite beautiful enough to put at the front of the house. It can be used as a central plume in a winter hanging basket out of doors. Again the colour is at its best and most cheerful during the winter, the green leaves being set off by a fine shocking-pink broad main rib and stem. The plants will go on until you tire of them or eat them, or until they grow too leggy as they come up to flower. I have grown them on in a very big tub right through the following summer, finding it necessary to stake the heavy head of flowers. The young plants make an unusual setting for bulbs and golden-foliaged or winter flowering ericas (heathers) and I really cannot speak too highly of them, along with the flower cabbages and kales.

Grown from a packet of seed, the stalks and broad mid-rib of chard are eaten as sea kale and the leaves as spinach. You need not spoil the display if you frugally take off a few outer leaves at a time for cooking. There is also a chard with a lettuce-green leaf and a white mid-rib, equally striking over a lengthy period, which can be cooked in the same way.

Even a dwarf apple tree can be grown in a big tub. Some nurserymen offer young trees on a

Tomatoes for summer salads can be successfully grown in pots. They also add an extra flourish of green to the patio or balcony.

dwarf root stock, which encourages early fruiting, with a very dwarf habit and small roots. They do need staking, but can be trained into dwarf pyramids, espalier, or cordon shapes, just like ordinary apple trees. Also available to be grown in tubs on balconies, roof gardens, and so on, are 'Family trees' which consist of three varieties of apple or three of pear grafted on one tree. They make an evenly-balanced bush. As the growers point out, should you move house within six years of planting you can take your orchard with you!

Grow asparagus

There is no reason why in a very big box you should not grow the lovely and delicious asparagus. The foliage is light and airy, it has red berries in late summer, and if you are patient for several years you will be magically rewarded with sticks big enough to eat. Asparagus really does need a very rich compost and regular feeding and watering. In a big window box you could grow it with sweet peas, for asparagus foliage is often cut to go with sweet pea flowers.

Though I have never tried them personally, figs are said to do well when grown in pots, enjoying the restriction of the roots. Hardy vines are also said to fruit well in a tub. I have, however, grown the ornamental purple-leafed vine which gives decorative little fruits.

I can see no good reason why raspberries, loganberries, and other soft fruits should not be grown in large containers.

There are so many herbs which make very satisfactory window box plants, and I have even grown some in wall baskets where space was at a premium. You may like the gold and silverleaved forms of thyme as well as the familiar green, and there are both white and pink flowered forms. All make pleasant additions to small container gardens and are also excellent for lining hanging baskets. Devoted cooks add thyme to stews, casseroles, and cheese and egg dishes. Parsley, which is said 'to go to the devil and back' before it comes up can have its germination speeded up slightly if after sowing you water it once with boiling water. It will grow in either shade or sun, and must not be allowed to dry out.

Pot marjoram can be produced in a big box or

tub, and the golden form makes a delightful foliage plant. This is a perennial but can be kept neat by trimming back. It likes full sun. Chives make a green grassy crop, with very pleasant purple drumstick flowers. The leaves are delicious chopped in salads, served on scrambled egg, and so on. The subtle onion flavour is said to ease coughs and colds. Chives are supposed to cure black spot on roses, so may be worth planting in association with miniature roses in containers. Again, in bigger containers grow yellow or purple forms of sage as well as the green which is traditional in stuffing for duck and with pork dishes. If pruned hard back in spring, sage can be kept within bounds.

There are dwarf lavenders and ones with pink, white, or deep purple flowerheads. Control the growth by clipping back in spring. The flowers can be picked and dried for fragrant use in pot-pourri, lavender bags, etc.

Ruta (rue) Jackman's Blue makes lovely neat mounds of blue-grey. The bitter flavour of the filigree leaves makes it unsuitable for cooking but it is very decorative. It is reputed to have medicinal properties; years ago people used to make 'rue tea' as a kind of cure-all.

Pieces of mint will quickly grow roots in water in summer. There are many sorts — apple mint, peppermint, variegated green and white mints, all of which are easy to grow as container plants.

A range of white plastic pots each holding a different herb keeps the spreaders such as mint in their rightful place and can look well edging steps or on a ledge, perhaps by the kitchen door.

Worth thinking about if you become really keen on growing greenhouse-type crops, but have no space for a real greenhouse, are the miniature

glass houses now available to stand against a sunny wall. These are ideal for a balcony, patio, or terrace, and will accommodate plant boxes or growing bags. The Victorians used similar glass structures outside a suitable window.

Finally, two very useful kitchen crops which can be grown in big outdoor containers are courgettes and special cucumbers offered by nurserymen specifically for outdoor cultivation. Courgettes are raised from seed; sow the seed singly in 3 inch peat pots in a warm place in April. Plant outside in late May, or you can sow directly outside in May. Most courgettes are green, but there is a yellow one available which would look good in a window box. Courgette plants take up a lot of space, and one per window box would probably be enough unless your boxes are enormous.

Outdoor varieties of cucumbers are grown from seed sown from January to May in good seed compost with one seed to a $2\frac{1}{2}$ inch pot. Warm, moist conditions are necessary to get the young plants established. Water the pot and cover it with a plastic bag; a shelf over a radiator or in an airing cupboard could supply the heat. Plant out in late May. Alternatively, you can sow the seeds directly outdoors in late May. Particularly suitable for container cultivation are Patio-Pik (which the seedsmen point out takes up no more room than a cabbage) and Pot Luck. Both are compact hybrids. Patio-Pik should, even if neglected, produce 30 or more cucumbers per plant. It is an early producer. Pot Luck I particularly recommend for tubs, patio pots, and window boxes.

A town gardener can grow tomatoes along a deep window ledge.

9

MORE PLANTS...
AND FEWER PESTS

Gardeners were ever optimists. Before we come to plant up our containers, whatever sort they are, we see them in the mind's eye awash with fabulous blooms, festooned with opulent colour. But when we come to cost the plants required it is a yearly shock, perhaps a setback, to find how expensive they are to buy nowadays. We cannot blame the nurserymen. Raising plants commercially these days is a constant headache, with heavy expense involved. Wages for staff have to be found, the rates, lighting, heating, composts, pots, and other overheads all have to be covered. It is easy enough to say 'Oh yes, but how easy it is to raise plants from seed or by division – he must be made of money'. It is, but also what the amateur never takes into account, and to which he need not put a price, is his own time. The nurseryman has to charge for time.

With this in mind I have written this chapter, certainly with the main aim of economy but also because it is often a great pleasure and satisfaction to see sturdy plants growing away which we have raised from a packet of insignificant brown seed or a cutting given by a friend. There is nothing, I have found, brings gardening friends closer than the interchange of plants. And this costs little, or nothing at all. I always raise a few more plants than I need for myself in order to be able to give some away. When giving someone cuttings in a plastic bag, dash a little splash of water inside the

Flowers make a welcome up the steps.

bag first of all to provide humidity. Put the cuttings inside, blow into the bag to hold it open like a balloon, and tie up the top firmly. Cuttings and young plants should be handled with care at all times.

Raising plants from seed

One might think that raising plants from seed would be the easiest thing in the world. But thousands of packets of embryo flowers are inadvertantly 'lost' every year. For one thing, plenty are never even sown! That's a common fault with many women who buy them and forget them, but as a friend of mine remarked 'They won't grow in the packet'. True, but thousands of people are lured by the picture on the packet or in the catalogue, buy the seeds, put them away 'until planting time', then forget all about them. I think this may be due partly to their being displayed in the shops and garden centres too early in the year. The seeds which will be of most interest to us as container gardeners are perhaps the hardy and half-hardy annuals – subjects which flower the same year as they are sown, then die. We must sow seed again next year if we want them again. Some, like the nasturtium, will provide us with plenty of seed for the following summer, and the seed should be collected when ripe and carefully stored in a cool, dry place until sowing time.

Hardy annuals are sown in spring straight into the containers where they are to remain. Half-hardy annuals can be sown and raised in a sunroom, garden frame, or greenhouse, from which frost can be completely excluded, and then planted out into the containers when all danger of frost is past. Study seedsmen's catalogues – they are always most helpful and informative – and the instructions printed on the seed packets themselves. They will tell you which plants are hardy or half-hardy and give instructions on sowing and rearing. Any marked 'F.1' hybrid are specially recommended. Pelleted seed, though costing a little more than ordinary seed, can be an advantage. It is very easy to sow, for every pellet contains one seed which is easy to see and handle and thus easy to sow in the place where it is wanted. Pellets can be placed the right distance apart, avoiding the need for thinning out and transplanting. Seedsmen say plants grown from pelleted seed develop a higher tolerance to drought, and growth is not checked because

transplanting is not necessary. Keep well watered until they germinate.

You may, of course, have things growing in your containers – spring bulbs, for instance – at the same time as the seed of annuals could be sown, in early spring. If you have no system of interchangeable containers, you will need to sow seed in pots or seedboxes to get them coming along. Otherwise you can always wait until your containers are cleared and sow seeds as late as June, but this obviously means the flowers will be later.

For raising seeds I use John Innes Compost No. 1, or the specially made individual peat pots which are available for raising seed. When the small plants are large enough to handle – about 2 or 3 inches high – they should be thinned out and spaced at about 6 inches apart.

I was interested last year when my sister, who is a particularly keen container gardener, bought a number of young fibrous rooted begonia plants which were in small polystyrene boxes in which they had been raised, each box being only about 2 inches by 6 inches. 'You will have to divide those plants,' we all told her when she brought them home from the church sale. But she was adamant that she wanted to try an experiment in growing them on in the same boxes. Her argument was that she had not much room on the flower-packed shelves of her glazed porch and thought they would 'just grow small flowers'. In fact, the experiment was very successful. The overcrowded little plants bloomed small but confounded all the experts by flowering prolifically right into the autumn. She is a very good container gardener, of course, and gives her plants top-notch attention, but considering that these plants were not given any feed, and their roots must have been terribly cramped, they thrived miraculously.

Experts scoff at such goings-on, but doing the unconventional thing often comes off. This particular idea might be worth copying if you do not have a lot of room, or if you prefer smaller flowers, so long as you remember to water regularly and, I would suggest, feed once a week. Another of my sister's notions was to grow a trailing lobelia as a standard, training it up a stick instead of letting it trail. It made a most unusual and charming plant.

But to get back to seed raising – when plants raised in pots or seedboxes are ready to go into the containers, tap the box sharply to loosen the soil and remove the young plants gently, handling each by its top not by the root. Similarly, when removing a young plant from a pot, tap the pot sharply against something hard and then let the plant and its root ball drop into your waiting hand. After planting in the container, water well. I like to choose a damp or showery day for the job if possible.

Some plants normally thought of, and grown as, annuals can survive the winter in a frost-free environment, petunias and lobelia, for instance. I find they make splendid plants the following year, coming into bloom early.

Hardy biennials

If you think of the word 'biennial' as 'bi-annual' you will remember that this means two years, for a biennial plant sown as seed in spring or early summer comes into flower not that same year, like an annual, but the following year. It includes such favourites as wallflowers (cheiranthus in the

catalogues sometimes), foxglove, dwarf Sweet Williams, etc. Seed can be sown early in heat indoors, but I prefer to sow in seedboxes outside in May–June, transplanting the plants into their flowering containers later in the year (September–October). They will stand fast and come through the winter safely out of doors.

Perennials

A perennial is a happy plant which grows on for a number of years, certainly more than just one or two. Perennials, too, can be raised from seed if you have the patience, otherwise they are the easiest thing in the world to increase by dividing

So many beautifully coloured geraniums from which to choose.

one root to make a number of new plants. I have found the easiest method of splitting is to plunge two garden forks back to back through the centre of the plant and then firmly lever them apart with their long handles.

Home propagators

There are all kinds of small home propagators on the market, both for raising seeds and cuttings, some with special heating arrangements if you want to go in for this in a big way. I have found the small plastic rooting bags, specially designed for rooting cuttings, are ideal and attractive enough for the bags to sit on a window ledge or kitchen worktop, out of bright sunshine. You can raise up to 15 plants at a time this way. Everything is explained on the bag, and there are even dotted lines to show exactly where to cut the plastic for inserting the cuttings and watering. In the summer, when days are warm, geraniums will root within a few days, and within a few weeks make good little plants ready for putting into containers.

These rooting bags can be used a number of times, and certainly long enough to be able to satisfy the average person's needs and provide a few extra plants to give away or exchange for other plants with friends. Another way which I have found successful for cuttings is to insert them all the way round a pot of good soil, putting the whole thing, after watering, inside a large polythene bag. Dipping the ends of the cuttings in water and then into one of the special hormone rooting powders assists speedy rooting.

The easiest cuttings to take from shrubs are perhaps those obtained by pulling off a side shoot with a strong downward movement which will come away with what is called a 'heel'. Cut back any raggedness with a sharp knife, dip into hormone rooting powder, and plant in a pot. Any leaves low on the cutting should be removed.

Geranium cuttings

When taking a cutting of a geranium (pelargonium), cut off a shoot of about 4 inches long from the growing plant with a sharp knife. Make the cut immediately below a node, which is the bit where the leaf joins the stem, for cuttings root easily from here. Cut away all the leaves except those at the growing tip. Place the cuttings into a mixture of equal amounts of silver sand and moist peat, or into a growing bag. Do not plant the cutting so deeply that its second node is covered. Geraniums are best left to root in warmth and, unlike most cuttings, do not like covering with a polythene bag.

Water only when the cuttings are really in need, and try to prevent water falling on the foliage, as this can lead to rotting. When roots have formed, the youngsters can be potted in John Innes No. 2 compost using 3-inch pots. At the same time, take out the growing tip, to ensure a bushy plant. Indeed, if you can brace yourself to nip back the sideshoots later on many more flower shoots will be produced, so giving just what we require – compact, stubby plants full of blooms, rather than skinny, leggy ones with only a few brave flowers on the ends of long stems. We can keep 'stopping' the plants in this way until around the end of May, when they can go into their permanent abodes and should be a fine sight within weeks, to delight us all summer long.

Cuttings, by the way, for flowering the following season are better if taken in August–September. If cuttings are taken with care from the parent plants it is possible they will not be missed, for the summer display will not be spoiled. Spring cuttings can be taken in March.

When space is scarce it is best to take cuttings in this way ready for next year's baskets and boxes. They take up far less room than the big, bushy parent plants at the end of the season and so it is easier to bring them safely through the winter. An indoor window ledge in a cool room which is safe from frost, but yet gets plenty of light, is ideal.

A paved front becomes a pleasing patio garden.

Three 5-inch pots holding five cuttings each will give you 15 plants for next summer's containers, and you can have more or fewer pots depending on your requirements. Stand them out of doors if you possibly can until the end of September. Give a liquid feed every week from January onwards. Plants should be 'hardened off' in early May. If you have a cold frame this means leaving the top off during the day, but if you are bringing the plants along indoors they can be put outside in a sheltered spot during the day and brought in at night. Put them into a cool room, of course, or the purpose is lost.

Do not be deceived by the mild, balmy days of May into putting the plants out into their permanent positions too early. Cold winds will make the leaves yellow, and our carefully-grown plants can be some months recovering from this harsh experience. Once planted and growing well, geraniums will flower best in sunny and even dryish conditions, though they must be fed and watered regularly. However, these ideal container plants will put up with more occasional neglect than most.

Propagating fuchsias

You can take various kinds of cuttings from the fuchsia. The easiest way, in spring or summer, is to cut off a shoot immediately below a pair of leaves about 3 inches down one of the stems. Remove the two lower leaves and you have a cutting ready to go into a pot; a number of cuttings can be planted all the way round the edge of a pot, as with geraniums. Use a very sharp knife when taking cuttings, to get a nice clean cut for best results. Semi-hardwood cuttings are quite different, being taken from the plant when the 'wood' is ripe and hard at the end of the summer. Pull off pieces of sideshoot growing from the main stem. Each piece should be about 5 inches long.

Cuttings from ivies

Remove portions about 3 inches long from the plant, again cutting below the spot where the leaf joins the stem. John Innes Potting Compost No. 1 can be used, again placing the cuttings all the way round the edge of a pot, or else inserting them into rooting bags which can be placed on an indoor window ledge. Cuttings take about five

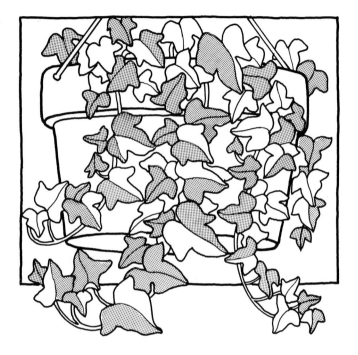

weeks to root. Look at an established ivy plant and you will notice that it has long trailing juvenile growths and bushy adult growths towards the top of the plant. Propagate from the young trails. The bushier adult foliage is more difficult to root, and surprisingly only ever produces the less attractive adult foliage.

When the plants have become really well rooted, grow them on in individual pots of John Innes No. 2 in a light place, and if you pinch back the growing shoots from time to time good plants with close bushy growth will be achieved. Plant out into their permanent homes when established. To make a charming hanging basket with all-the-year-round appeal fill your basket with moss and John Innes No. 2. Five ivy plants all the way round and one in the centre make a really effective show. Those ivies with small or medium sized foliage are best for both baskets and boxes. Each spring, trim the long trails back.

Petunias and bedding plants

Fuchsias, geraniums, and ivies are probably the main stand-bys for container gardeners, but many plants normally grown purely as annuals and thrown away in late summer, such as petunias, dwarf lobelias, snapdragons, and wallflowers may be easily reproduced vegetatively for filling containers the following year. One or more plants, depending on requirements and the space available, should be lifted, potted, and brought into a greenhouse or frost-free sunroom (in Surrey, in a south-facing glazed porch, I have had 100 per cent success) for the winter. Take cuttings as with other subjects and pot them into rooting bags or pots of light sandy soil in spring.

Dealing with pests

Most people do not give a thought to the possibility of pests until their baskets are in full swing and boxes burgeoning. Then one day, probably while watering, we may notice a sticky substance on some of the leaves and two days later it is clear we really have got greenfly. Or the birds we have fed all winter suddenly attack our early peeping primroses, nipping off all the buds, and it is obvious something must be done. Insect pests such as greenfly can be deterred greatly by routine weeding and good cultivation. A strongly growing plant will more easily cope in the early

stages of insect attack. Always take off every dead or dying leaf and flower.

Keep the plants clean and fresh with overhead spraying during dry spells. If only one plant is being attacked, it still pays to treat all the other plants in the same container at the same time. There are proprietary brands of sprays and powders on the market to deter most pests nowadays – including pepper dusts to put off cats! The big manufacturers seem to be constantly bringing out new products, so ask at your garden shop. I have found that an aerosol can is usually all that is required to deal with an insect attack, and this saves having to mix a large quantity of insecticide.

Many pests tend to hide under foliage, and so are very easily detected in hanging baskets and window boxes, where they are more visible than on plants in the garden. When only one or two plants are involved, you can even brace yourself to rub out greenfly and other insects by hand in the early stages of an attack. One of the few advantages of a windy site is that aphides are unlikely to be much of a problem.

Ants can be another problem. These pests, apart from the possibility that they may come indoors, do encourage aphides, often introducing them to plants, on which they 'farm' them. They also tunnel about in the soil of pots and boxes, make nests, and disturb root systems of plants, which often die as a result from lack of moisture. Fortunately there are proprietary ant killers available, and if you buy one sold for destroying ants in the home it will be non-poisonous.

Other pests you may find on plants in a container include red spider, whitefly, blackfly, and scale insects. You may not realise your plants have red spider, which are difficult to see, until foliage mottles and growth becomes deformed. In severe cases the mites spin tiny webs over the stems and leaves. Regular overhead spraying with water not only keeps the foliage clean but the addition of 1 teaspoonful of common salt to a gallon of water helps deter red spider. Sunroom gardeners often think the scale insects, which are small blister-like objects, are part of the plant itself, and I have known people watch with interest for some months to see what happens next! In fact, these insects are feeding on the plant.

Whitefly are related to both scale insects and aphides. Like minute white moths, they rise from the plant when disturbed and can be difficult to deter because they have five stages in their life cycle from egg to adult – you may think you have got rid of them at one stage but there may still be eggs waiting to hatch. Control with a pyrethrum-based product sprayed on two or three times a week for about a month.

It is a good general rule to take immediate steps against any insects you find on your plants, except ladybirds and bees. If not dealt with promptly, insect pests are unlikely to go away; on the contrary, they will increase and become more difficult to deal with.

The early spring can put the container gardener right off birds! And so, for that matter, can the summer, if you grow strawberries in a basket or tub out of doors. Many birds peck off buds and flowers and in the spring have been known to almost pick plants to pieces. So try to be one step ahead, particularly if you grow primroses and polyanthus. Buy a bundle of unobtrusive green-painted pot plant stakes and carefully slit down the top ½-inch of each. With these make a barricade all round the container or basket you wish to protect. Space them evenly and stretch black cotton, not thick thread (birds can get dangerously entangled in strong thread) between the stakes; criss-cross the cotton over the container. The idea is to deter the birds, which detest feeling with their legs or wings something they cannot see, not to trip them up! A covering of chicken wire over a container will deter cats, where these are a problem.

Where slugs and snails are concerned, I find the best answer is Liquid Sluggit, which gets right down to the business when watered on. It kills the pests beneath the soil as well as on top.

Plant diseases

Botrytis is a fungus or grey-coloured mould which thrives in moist conditions, usually first attacking old discarded leaves. It is an obvious advantage to keep all plants in a clean condition as a first line of defence.

Damping off is when a young plant rots at soil level, by which time it is really too late to do anything about it. But resolve next time to use a sterile compost and not to over-water.

Mildew is due to lack of movement of the air and is therefore something which occurs with containers in very sheltered positions. This disease is easily recognisable, appearing as a thick grey dust over the surfaces of leaves.

Rust looks exactly like metal rust, and can attack fuchsias and geraniums as well as things like garden hollyhocks, on which it is commonly seen. In addition to controlling with a suitable spray treatment, take off and burn all affected leaves.

Proprietary treatments are available for dealing with all the common plant diseases which are likely to trouble the container gardener. As with pesticides, new products frequently come on the market so it is best to look and ask at a garden shop or the garden products counter at the chemist's.

Premature leaf-fall

When most of the leaves drop off a plant prematurely, or the leaves turn yellow, the reason may well be poor growing conditions. The soil may be too wet – or it may be too dry. The plant may not have been fed sufficiently, or it may be suffering from lack of light. The cause may even be that it has outgrown its container. Sudden alterations in temperature, particularly in spring, also cause leaf colour change. With these possibilities in mind the reason in a particular case should be obvious, and the remedy likewise.

None of these reasons necessarily means that the plant will die, though certainly it may be considerably weakened. In very severe cases, cut the plant back a little to see if it will shoot again. If and when it does shoot, mild feeding will aid its recovery.

10

A to Z
OF USEFUL PLANTS

It would be impossible to list all the plants, of many kinds, which will adapt happily to growing in containers of one sort or another. But here are some which I have found especially useful and attractive:

Ajuga (Bugle). Perennial creeping rosettes, mostly producing intense blue flower spikes of about six inches from May to July. Ajuga atropurpurea has bronze-purple leaves. Ajuga Burgundy Glow has lovely bronze-purple variegated foliage, while A. Pink Elf is a free-flowering pink form of about four inches. Likes sun or partial shade.

Alchemilla mollis (Lady's Mantle). Easy to grow, this favourite with flower arrangers makes a refreshingly light and airy effect in a reasonably sized box and is pretty in a basket. Pale green pleated leaves catch and hold drops of water after a shower of rain or overhead watering, and make a lovely setting for the froth of dainty lime-green flowers that go up to about 18 inches. Flowers and leaves are an excellent foil to any colour you put with them. For sun or shade.

Alyssum. Alyssum saxatile Citrinum is a very attractive pale yellow form of the ever-popular alyssum. A. Flore Pleno is a double form, and A. Compactum is a bright gold form. Try alyssum for an unusual springtime hanging basket. Will grow in sun or partial shade.

Anthemis (Camomile). I have particularly liked anthemis cupaniana, which makes ferny mounds of silver-grey foliage and carries for months on end large white 'daisies', from May. Cut out stems after they flower and the plant will bloom again in late summer. Strikes easily from cuttings, and is happy in full sun or semi-shade. A perennial, it stays attractive all winter with its grey foliage.

Arabis. Arabis Flore Pleno is a 'must' for hanging baskets and window boxes, carrying double white stock-like flowers April–May. A. variegata has handsome variegated rosettes all winter, and white flowers in spring. Suitable for sunny or semi-shaded positions.

Arenaria balearica. These small, moss-like plants have tiny white star-like flowers in summer. Plants which I have found make excellent linings for hanging baskets. Evergreen. A. purpurascens has purple foliage.

Armeria (Thrift). This tussocky plant I have used as a basket liner and it makes an attractive edging to a box also. Evergreen, covered in summer with drumsticks of pink. A. Corsica has brick-red flowers. A. maritima splendens Alba has white flowers.

Artemisia. The smaller kinds make charming earth-coverers. A. lanata is a prostrate one with silver filigree leaves, and A. schmidtii Nana is also attractive through which crocus and other bulbs will push their way.

Arum. Arum italicum marmoratum makes a fascinating subject for a window box or patio planter. Its winter leaves are marbled green and white. The leaves die down in summer but striking spikey seedheads of green ripening to orange begin to form in late July. Fresh foliage appears for the winter. The seedheads are poisonous, so plant out of children's reach.

Aubrieta (often spelled aubretia). There are

many named varieties of this popular spring flower, which I have even used for lining hanging baskets. A. Bressingham Red is a good large-flowered form. A. Bressingham Pink is a good double. A. Dr. Mules is a fine purple, and A. marginata variegata has green foliage prettily edged with white, and blue flowers.

Aucuba (Spotted Laurel). Planted in a sunny position, the yellow colour of the heavily splashed and spotted evergreen leaves makes this a suitable and popular shrub for a winter box while the plants are still small.

Azalea. Dwarf varieties are delightful shrubs for window boxes, which can be easily filled with the lime-free soil they require. The evergreen kinds are a distinct advantage. There are many colours of flowers available, to fit in with most colour schemes. Never allow them to dry out; peat used as a mulch is of benefit. The larger azaleas can be accommodated in suitably sized patio planters, etc.

Begonia. Richly-coloured tuberous begonias flower freely and make excellent subjects for container gardening. Pendulous sorts are ideal for hanging baskets. There are varieties that are frilled and crested. Begonias are mostly bought as dry tubers, although they can be raised from seed. Start tubers off indoors in a warm room in pots in mid-March; by the middle of May they should be hardened off ready to plant in containers. Fibrous-rooted begonias (semperflorens) I have found best grown from pelleted seed, but they are readily available as plants. Some have very attractively coloured foliage. Begonias like a partially shady place and should not go outdoors until all danger of frost is past. The compost must not become too dry or buds will fall.

Bellis (Daisy). This plant is charming in springtime containers. Dresden China is a popular double pink button daisy of miniature size, and Rob Roy is a little taller (about 6 inches) and a red button. Remove all spent flowers immediately so that the plants do not set seed; divide the plants regularly. A delightful perennial.

Bergenia. These valuable evergreen foliage plants are useful all the year round in boxes and tubs for their splendid leaf shapes. Some have leaves which redden in late summer, and all have good branching heads of flowers in the spring. Try B. Ballawley in a big planter; it has large green summer foliage, and rosy pink flowers in spring (and possibly a few in early autumn). B. Silberlicht, with white flowers, and B. beesiana purpurascens, whose leaves colour very well in winter, are both attractive. Sun or shade.

Calendula (Marigold). A hardy annual. Geisha Girl has large orange flowers. C. Art Shades has a wonderful range of colours, with creams, apricots, oranges.

Campanula (Bell Flower). There is a wide variety of small campanulas, mostly bought for colour in the rock garden during the summer, but I use many of them in my hanging baskets, planting them in the sides, where they quickly form a neat covering. C. Blue Clips is a dwarf blue

with flowers on 4-inch stems, and C. White Clips is white. C. E.H. Frost is an enchanter with pure white bells and a trailing habit. C. isophylla has for many years been a favourite for summer hanging baskets indoors but the plant, which is in fact hardy in many parts of Britain, makes a very good outdoor display in every kind of container; it can be allowed to trail or be staked and grown as an upright. Both white and blue forms are available and white is lovely with blue trailing lobelia in a basket.

Carnations.   Pendulous carnations can be raised from seed to flower within five months of sowing. They come mainly in pinks and reds. All carnations and pinks bought in as plants will trail if you do not stake them, however.

Chlorophytum.   For indoor hanging baskets all the year round, or outdoors in summer, this is the very popular green-and-white-striped foliage plant. It throws out new little plants on long stems as runners, giving a waterfall effect.

Cobaea scandens (Cathedral Bells). This is a frost-tender graceful climber, flowering from July onwards in a sunny position. The flowers are green-violet bells. Sow seed indoors in early spring. Normally grown as an annual out of doors, but in a cool greenhouse or conservatory will be perennial.

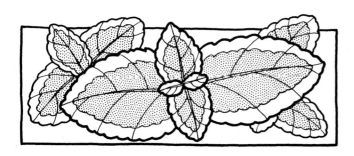

Colchicum. Often mistakenly called autumn crocus, these are large corms with big crocus-like flowers. C. Water Lily has huge many-petalled blooms of pale purple. C. autumnale (meadow saffron) is pale rose or white. C. byzantinum has up to 20 lilac-rose flowers in a spathe. Colchicum are sometimes offered for sale to grow on window ledges out of soil, which shows how easy they are. After flowering they should be removed from window boxes, but may be left in larger planters, as they produce very large leaves in spring which must be left on until they die down naturally in June or July. Sun or shade.

Coleus. Foliage plants from seed in a fantastic range of colours. They require sufficient sunlight if the colours are to stay bright. Pieces will root easily in water. All flowers, which are not very attractive, should be pinched out. C. Carefree is a good compact and bushy variety, and those called Dragon Coleus have bright scarlet leaves edged with gold. They grow well in tubs and window boxes from early summer; take cuttings, or bring plants indoors before the frosts.

Cosmos. Prettily-coloured daisy flowers held above dainty foliage. Normally grown in a border, but they do make delightful subjects for tubs. Raise from seed, and plant out in May. If not allowed to dry out they will give a long period of bloom.

Crocus. These cheap and cheerful friends of early spring are great value for money. They hug boxes and baskets like a coverlet only inches high. The winter-flowering group bloom as early as February. Choose from such species as C. chrysanthus Lady Killer (violet-blue with milky white), C. Golden Bunch (which gives 18 to 24 flowers from a single bulb), C. Cloth of Gold (yellow with dark purple feathering), and C. vernus Vanguard (a lovely shade of pale mauve with flowers in profusion a fortnight before the ordinary large crocus). There are also autumn-flowering crocus available, attractive but with smaller flowers than colchicum.

Daffodils and narcissi. If your window box or other container is very much exposed to the wind, go for miniatures or the shorter-stemmed kinds. The fine trumpet daffodil called Youth has large deep golden yellow flowers, and goes up to about 12 inches tall. The double flowered daffodil Van Sion goes to about 13 inches. For large tubs and more sheltered sites, a collection of Mount Hood makes a magnificent show; the flowerheads are white, on 20-inch stems.

Dicentra spectabilis. There are a number of dicentras grown as hardy border plants but my favourite for a big terrace planter is D. spectabilis (sometimes known as Bleeding Heart, Dutchman's Breeches, and Lady in the Bath). The flower stems carrying the little hearts arch above the fine ferny foliage, with remarkable effect. Goes up to 2 feet high, and needs a deep rich soil.

Eccremocarpus (Chilean Glory Flower). I have found this to be a much-admired plant in hanging baskets. The vivid orange tubular flowers are produced on long trailing stems and are well set off by bright green leaves. After the flowers, interesting green, then black, seedpods appear. The stems are cut back to the base in late autumn. Not hardy – needs frost-free conditions in winter. Normally grown as a climber. Requires lots of water in the growing season. Can be raised from seed.

Epimedium (Bishop's Hat). These lovely foliage plants produce flowers in spring. The foliage is long-lasting and in a container makes a setting for other subjects. Perfectly hardy. There are a number of different kinds. E. rubrum, for example, is particularly effective when the new leaves emerge with their bronze-red colours. Epimedium Youngianum niveum has smaller leaves which come soft brown when new, and white flowers.

Erica (Heather). There are many fine kinds, with colourful year-round foliage, including copper yellow and grey as well as green. Ericas are very valuable for the top of hanging baskets, window boxes, and any other small raised gardens. Ideal for permanent plantings. Clip back after flowering, to keep compact in shape. Most need a lime-free soil. E. carnea Springwood White and Springwood Pink are not fussy as to a little lime, and have the added virtue of flowering in the winter no matter how hard the weather.

Euonymus. A number of good euonymus can be found, and with their likeable evergreen foliage they are all to be recommended for container cultivation. E. fortunei Gracilis has small green leaves edged with white and takes on a pleasing pink tinge in winter. The kind called Emerald'n'Gold is well described by its name, and like all euonymus is effective planted with dwarf conifers and shrubs or as the backing for flowering subjects. Striking when used as a trailing plant in a hanging basket. E. Silver Queen and E. Golden Prince (the latter a better colour in a sunny position) are both worth having.

Fatsia japonica (Castor Oil Plant). Young plants will supply window boxes or large planters with a handsome evergreen foliage shrub which will do well in any aspect. The glossy green leaves are something between a fig leaf and an ivy leaf in shape.

Fuchsia. Great favourites which provide a long period of colour. There are miniature sorts, trailers, and ones which may be grown as standards on single stems. Two hardy ones I can recommend are F. Empress of Prussia, which has a semi-prostrate habit, a dwarf which has large flowers of red and purple, and F. Eva Borg, which is cream and magenta. In the worst of the winter I always bring these under some cover, such as my porch. The majority of fuchsias are not hardy enough to survive winter outside everywhere, and must be wintered in a frost-free place. In spring prune the plants back to one or two buds per shoot, and plant one to each hanging basket, or in tubs or boxes. To keep the plants shapely, 'summer pruning' can be undertaken by pinching back side shoots to produce a bushy plant. If given plenty of root room they remain much longer in flower. F. magellanica gracilis variegata is a dainty cream pink and green variegated leaf fuchsia which is very hardy.

Geraniums (hardy) (See also pelargoniums). The true geranium is a hardy border plant, some of the smaller kinds of which can be invaluable for baskets, window boxes, and pots. The larger make fine subjects for tubs. G. Claridge Druce (18 inches) has lilac-pink flowers and fresh green foliage. G. Endressii A.T. Johnson (about 12 inches) has silvery-pink flowers. G. Russell Prichard (6 inches) has a creeping habit and reddish flowers, while G. Renardii (9 inches) has pleasantly marked white blooms and unusual grey-green foliage which can make a quiet feature with other flowers. G. macrorrhizum variegatum (12 inches) has frilly leaves prettily variegated cream and green. All are happy in sun or shade, except for the variegated one, which will colour better in good light.

Grasses. It may seem a little odd to suggest planting grasses in a container but there are some highly colourful ones available which make excellent foils for flowers or foliage plants. Festuca amethystina (glauca) is a good-looking really blue grass when grown in full sun and dry soil. It makes about 8 inches in height. Acorus gramineus variegatus presents neat little evergreen hummocks. Milium effusum Aureum, often called Bowles' Golden Grass, has bright lime-yellow foliage in spring and summer even in shade, and clouds of matching flowers. Pennisetum orientale has memorable lavender-pink fluffy seedheads. In a box, these grasses are easily managed and may be divided into small clumps each spring. All make an unusual top to a hanging basket, with or without other plants.

Hedera (Ivy). These relatively pest-free plants are ideal for container gardening. They may take a little time to settle in, but once established they gallop away and need a fairly fierce pruning out every year, pruning out in the sense that it is often necessary to take out whole trails right back to base in spring. A gentle clip over may also become necessary. The effect should be that of a neat, controlled (long or short) hair-do rather than a shaggy, unkempt mop. An urn or similar container achieves a very romantic look if an ivy is allowed to cascade over the rim. An interesting effect can be made for a roof or terrace garden by planting ivies in tubs and training them up tall stakes and then along loops of cord or fine chain swung between the stakes. On the whole it will be the smaller-foliaged types which will prove most useful for containers. There are many lovely variegated kinds, easily available, and a very pleasant idea is to group several in a mixed planting. H. Helix Buttercup is a slow-growing ivy with good gold leaves. H. Helix Goldheart (Jubilee) has a gold heart displayed in the centre of

In a setting of pink roses and grey-green ballota, this old stone sink with its stonecrops, gently decorates an outdoor terrace the year around.

pleasant schemes to go with every kind of house decoration are possible. In the slight protection of my glazed porch, which has a door, I find they make a delicious display in long boxes and a hanging basket from as early as January. I plant up two boxes, one a month later than the other, so that I have months of continuity of blooming, removing the first box when it finally goes out of flower. Hyacinths can be planted in August, September, and October. I keep them in the dark, or outside on a bed of ashes and covered with ashes. If you don't have ashes use black polythene and a few slug pellets. Bring them out when they are well rooted and the flower spikes begin to show, and gradually introduce them to the light. I put mine in the porch and cover them with a double thickness of newspaper for a few days.

Impatiens (Busy Lizzie). These frost-tender subjects, normally seen indoors as pot plants, make wonderful items for hanging baskets, window boxes, and other containers, growing much larger than usual when in a large container. They have a very long period in bloom and I cannot speak too highly of them. There are many dazzling colours, but one of my own favourite boxes is always made up of white petunias and white Busy Lizzies, seen against a sea-green house wall. You can either buy the plants or they can be raised from seed sown early in the year.

Lamium (Deadnettle). Lamium maculatum Beacon Silver is a quick-growing, outstanding plant with silver-white creeping foliage. L. maculatum aureum is a good golden leaf form and a useful plant for cool conditions, as indeed all the lamiums are very easy to please. L. maculatum Shell Pink has green and white variegated leaves and shell-pink flowers.

each triangular green leaf. H. Glacier has grey and white variegation; H. Green Ripple has dark green jagged foliage which gives the effect of rippling movement.

Helleborus. Helleborus corsicus I have found invaluable in a large planter, and have even seen it growing in a big window box. It is tough all the year round, with evergreen foliage from which in early spring pale apple-green 'flowers' appear; these stand for many months.

Hyacinth. Buy one colour or two at most for great impact. The colour range is good, and

Liriope. Liriope muscari has dark evergreen foliage in clumps, but it is in the autumn when its grape-hyacinth-like violet-coloured flowers appear that it really becomes a quiet eye-catcher. Hardy. Sun or shade.

Lithospermum. Lithospermum Heavenly Blue is a delightful plant with vivid blue trailing flowers in spring. A lime-hater, it likes a sandy soil with peat or leaf-mould, and a position in full sunshine. It is hardy.

Lobelia. There are many annual sorts to grow other than the trailing and compact blues. L. Red Cascade is a trailer with purple-red flowers which have a white eye. L. Crystal Palace, which although it has deep royal blue flowers has bronze foliage that is interesting. L. Pumila Snowball is pure white. Buy L. String of Pearls and you get a mixture of colours.

Lonicera. Although the general run of honeysuckles can be grown in large tubs, I commend Lonicera nitida Baggesens Gold. This little shrubby species has yellow-green foliage which is evergreen and can be clipped into almost any shape and size. I even grow it on a single stem as a standard, clipped to a ball shape at the top. A pair of these can be a feature in tubs either side of a door if kept regularly clipped in the growing season. You can also get a little clipped-hedge effect in a window box. Grows easily from cuttings.

Nasturtium. Called Tropaeolum in catalogues. There are trailing kinds available, and others of more compact growth. T. Alaska Mixed is a super selection of assorted nasturtium colours, sold as seed, with the added attraction of green and white marbled foliage, making it pleasing from the moment the first leaves appear. T. Whirlybird Mixed make excellent container plants, with

Begonias of all kinds make ideal plants for every kind of container — indoors or out.

more flowers than foliage; the blooms are held well above the leaves, and there is a bright, country look.

Pansy (Viola in catalogues). Every kind of container looks better for a few cheerful pansies. I grow them even in hanging baskets and wall pots. V. cornuta, in either the purple-blue or white form, is normally grown as a border plant but makes an excellent subject for a hanging basket. Grow V. Blue Heaven if you want a good blue pansy; V. Lavender Lass for soft lavender; V.

Paper White, pure white; and V. Floral Dance mixed seed, which is very early flowering and will even bloom in mild spells during the winter.

Pelargonium (Usually called geraniums). Look out for the miniature, dwarf, trailing, variegated-foliaged, and coloured-leaf pelargoniums, some with single flowers, some with double. Plants which have been show-stoppers all summer must at the end of the season either be left for the first frosts to whisk them from us or have some provision made for their winter comfort. On lifting them from containers they may be found too big for the space you have available indoors; however, you can trim back the roots so that they will fit into a reasonably-sized pot of compost. Cut the plant back to about 5 inches above soil level, though it will be too late to take cuttings (which should be done August–September). Keep the over-wintering plants just moist and frost-free in a light window and they will begin to shoot in late winter. The first feed of the year can be a general fertiliser. After this, a good geranium feed high in potash is valuable, and the feed used for tomatoes is excellent, making the plants sturdy and also intensifies the colours of leaves and flowers. It is really well worth while feeding pelargoniums. The following are among my favourites, Silver Kewense, which is cream and green; Sunrocket (golden foliage); Chelsea Gem (pink flowers); and Irene (crimson blooms). There are very many kinds – it is worthwhile visiting a good pelargonium nursery to make your choice. Worth searching for are Sussex Lace (Crocodile), an ivy-leaf pelargonium whose green foliage is dappled with cream, and pink flowers, excellent for a basket; Gigi, which is the Swiss window box favourite; Show Girl, a sharp rich pink which is very floriferous right through the year; and Mrs. Henry Cox, a gay red, gold, and cream tricolour leaf with salmon blooms. Some F1 hybrids can be raised quickly from seed.

Petunia. I always grow petunias and find them invaluable for a long period of flower. They often bloom better in containers than in the open garden. They are grown from seed, or young plants can be bought. Although petunias are frost-tender and normally grown as annuals, I have managed to keep them for up to three years in my glazed porch. There are hundreds of varieties on the market, doubles and singles, and although a hanging petunia is offered in at least one catalogue I find that most petunias will in fact hang when sufficiently well-grown, if not staked.

Plectranthus. Normally grown as a house plant, plectranthus makes an excellent subject for a hanging basket. P. fruticosus is one of the easiest. Grown for its foliage, one plant in a hanging basket has been known to grow as much as 10 feet in a season. Excellent for a sunroom, conservatory, or sheltered balcony, as is P. coleoides marginatus, which produces rich green leaves with white veining, and pink flowers. Plants can be cut back if they become too large, and cuttings will root very easily in water. Plectranthus will put up with quite a lot of neglect, but not tolerate frost.

Ruta (Rue, the 'Herb of Grace'). R. graveolens Jackman's Blue makes a pungent but shapely little bush with glaucus blue leaves which are almost evergreen. Can be clipped over in early spring to keep it compact, and for the same reason the small, insignificant yellow flowers which appear in summer can be removed. There is a variegated sort with blue-green foliage streaked with creamy white. Both do well in a sunny position.

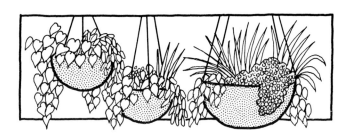

Sedum (Stonecrops). The sedum family includes both alpine and hardy perennial kinds. All cannot be bettered for our purpose. S. spectabile, the most commonly grown, is an ever-interesting container plant, with its glaucous leaves, even manner of growth, bright pink, red, or white flowers, and brown seedheads which, if left on all winter, continue the pleasing picture. Sedum spectabile Autumn Joy is superb. The small carpeting stonecrops can be useful for lining baskets or carpeting other containers. S. maximum atropurpureum has deep purple foliage, while S. Bressingham Purple has fine fleshy purple leaves and is perhaps even better than the former.

Sempervivum (Houseleeks). These have a special place in the container garden and I think it is not generally realised what a very large selection of coloured rosettes is to be had, from ones with silver cobwebs to big mahogany-red ones. All have the added bonus of not only being hardy and keeping their foliage through the winter but also producing very attractive summer flowers.

Stachys. S. lanata Silver Carpet (lamb's ear) is a good 'lamb's lug' for those who do not want the flowers to spoil the neat effect of the foliage, for this stachys hardly ever blooms. Good in a dry, sunny position as an under-planting to brightly-coloured geraniums etc. Stachys byzantinus has larger woolly foliage than Silver Carpet.

Tanacetum. Tanacetum densum amanum (this used to be called chrysanthemum haradjani) is an enchanter, making a low covering of silver-white leaves like tiny feathers. Ever-grey and hardy, and particularly pleasing when planted in a terracotta container.

Tellima. Tellima grandiflora purpurea is a good foliage plant for the whole year, which colours to bronze and reddish shades in winter. The green flowers in summer are rather insignificant but interesting. In big containers, can be used in association with slightly taller and differently coloured evergreens such as dwarf conifers.

Thyme. I have used some of the smaller dense mat-forming thymes as liners for hanging baskets, but the coloured foliage ones are most attractive hanging over the edge of any container. Thymus Doone Valley is a very striking thyme, having rich green foliage spangled with gold. T. citriodorus Aureus is an upright-growing sort with golden leaves. Thyme likes a dry, sunny position, and all will flower.

Tradescantia (Wandering Jew). These easily

A winter basket of hardy vinca with variagated leaves.

grown indoor pot plants have both silver and golden striped forms, and if a plant is grown in a light position the leaves will be tinged with pink or lavender. They grow away very strongly, and are thus useful for summer baskets though it should be remembered that they like plenty of water. Ideal for porches, sheltered terraces, sunrooms etc, in summer.

Vinca (Periwinkle). The periwinkle is not used sufficiently, it seems to me, in containers, where it will thrive even in shade, producing trails of light leafage all year round, with flowers into the bargain in spring and summer. V. major variegata has variegated foliage splashed with cream and gold. V. minor alba aurea variegata has leaves which are yellow, and white flowers, and is actually said to be best in a north or east facing situation.

Yucca. There are a number of yuccas, all of which I find the most tolerant plants imaginable for providing magnificent spikey heads of classic shape for the centre of a large urn or garden pot. They look particularly well planted in a raised position on a plinth or base, with the plant surrounded by trailing ivies. Hot and dry, they really do not seem to mind, and they will stand the winter, though they flower only rarely when confined to a container.

Zebrina. A plant which is sometimes confused with tradescantia, but it is larger and its leaves are more colourful. It has the same trailing habit but is rather slower-growing. The leaves have vivid purple underneath, making this a superb plant for a hanging basket. The top side of the leaves is purple and silver. Frost-tender and normally seen as an indoor pot plant, but easy to propagate by rooting stems.

Zygocactus (Christmas Cactus). Z. truncatus has flat leaf-life stems which resemble crab claws. It makes an excellent winter basket subject in a frost-free environment. It flowers lavishly, producing many cyclamen-pink blooms around Christmas and onwards. My experience is that it flowers most freely if watered only moderately during the summer and more freely during the flowering period.

Annuals from seed

By raising a few annuals from seed many new and 'different' effects can be won for our containers. From a host of lovely things I can recommend to you Ageratum Blue Blazer and Summer Snow, Aquilegia (columbine) Dragonfly Hybrids and Antirrhinum (snapdragon) Floral Cluster. This last snapdragon blooms early and is particularly resistant to the weather, while A. Humming Bird is an excellent dwarf mixture.

Aster Lilliput Mixed is an attractive aster with double flowers which goes up to about 12 inches. A. Pinocchio Mixed is even more dwarf and my only grumble is that proper colour schemes are difficult with mixed seedlings. I wish the seedsmen would sort them out further for us.

Balsam extra dwarf Tom Thumb Mixed is very free with its flowers (8 inches), and I have much liked Celosia plumosa (Prince of Wales Feathers) with its brilliant red or golden feathers; Dwarf Mixed, if you like a mixture and Fairy Fountains, another excellent colour range, is a little taller at 12 inches.

Annual chrysanthemums are always a favourite and I like Little Silver Princess which goes up to 18 inches for planters. Its flowers are white but for bigger containers do try Flame Shades and Suttons Special Mixture. Coxcomb (Celosia) Jewel Box Mixed (6 inches), Coleus Red Velvet and Eschscholzia (Californian Poppy) Miniature Primrose (5 inches) are other invaluable plants for inhabiting hanging baskets and boxes.

A friend of mine was extremely happy the year she grew Heliotrope or Cherry Pie in her window boxes for the perfume of the violet flowers, which she planted with dwarf single yellow dahlias, was a delight. Another year she tried an annual I had not seen before, Nemophila (Baby Blue Eyes) with white pansies and has plans next year for boxes of Phlox drummondii Twinkles which will fill the containers with a 7 inch high carpet.

I am very fond of poppies and already have plans to grow Papaver Alpine Mixed in matching baskets and boxes. Imagine 8-inch poppies peeping down over the edge of a low basket. Salpiglossis I have already tried and enjoyed them cascading their handsomely veined flowers out of the top of baskets.

For dramatic colour I suggest Salvia Red Hussar, Fireball (both about 12 inches) and Extra Dwarf Early Bird, another scarlet show stopper at about 9 inches. S. Compact Purple (12 inches again) with dwarf pink pelargoniums is another idea. Finally Zinnia Miniature Pompon Mixed at 9 inches and the coral Peter Pan Pink, rosy Peter Pan Plum and Peter Pan Scarlet make possible many original looking plantings so do try a few out for yourself.

INDEX

PLANT NAME/ALTERNATIVE	Pages	Spring	Summer	Autumn	Winter
Honeysuckle, *Lonicera*	26, 40, 91		W T		
Hop spp	14, 40		H T		
Hosta	64		T		
Houseleek, *Sempervivum*	22, 93	P W H	P W H	P W H	P W H
Hyacinth	21, 90	P W H			
Hydrangea	40, 58		T		
Immortelle, *Helichrysum*	22, 42		H		
Impatiens, *Busy Lizzie*	22, 90		H		
Ipomoea, *Morning Glory*	39		T		
Ivy spp, *Hedera*	80, 89	P W H	P W H	P W H	P W H
Japanese Aralia, *Fatsia japonica*	88	P T	P T	P T	P T
Kale	71		W		
Lady's Mantle, *Alchemilla*	64		W H	W H	
Lamb's Ears, *Stachys lanata*	22, 93	H	H	H	H
Lamium maculatum, *Dead Nettle*	22, 90		H		
Lavender	73	T			
Leopard's Bane, *Doronicum*	62	W T			
Lettuce	65, 67		W		
Lily	36, 38		T		
Liriope	90			W H	
Lithospermum, *Gromwell*	91		W H		
Lobelia	22, 81, 91		W H		
Loganberry	72		T		
Lonicera, *Honeysuckle*	26, 40, 91		W T		
Lychnis flos Jovis, *Campion*	54		W H		
Lysimachia, *Creeping Jenny*	22		H		
Maidenhair Fern, *Adiantum*	21, 63		H		
Marguerite	11, 25		H		
Marigold, *Calendula*	18, 86		P W H		
Megasea, *Bergenia*	54, 86	W T			
Mesembryanthemum	54		W H		
Mexican Aster, *Cosmos*	87		P H		
Mignonette	40		P W		
Mint	14, 61		P W H		
Morning Glory, *Ipomoea*	39		T		
Muscari, *Grape Hyacinth*	21	W H			
Narcissus	87	P W H			
Nasturtium *Tropaeolum*	22, 76, 91		P W H		
Nepeta, *Catmint*	54		W H		
Nertera depressa	43	H	H	H	H
Osmanthus	38	T	T	T	T
Pansy, *Viola*	21, 48, 91		W H T		
Parsley	61, 65	W H	W H	W H	W H
Passiflora, *Passion Flower*	40, 41		T		
Pelargonium, *Geranium*	53, 55, 92		W H		P
Pepper	69, 70		W T		
Periwinkle, *Vinca*	21, 94		W		
Petunia	22, 56, 92		P W H		
Polyanthus	24, 82	W H			
Poor Man's Orchid, *Schizanthus*	14, 22		H		
Pot Marigold, *Calendula*	18, 86		P W H		
Pot Marjoram	72		W		

P = Pot   W = Windowbox   T = Tub   H = Hanging basket